DROP
BY
DROP

Nourished by every unfolding of life

DROP BY DROP

Nourished by every unfolding of life

nomita kapur

STERLING PUBLISHERS (P) LTD.
Regd. Office: A1/256 Safdarjung Enclave, New Delhi-110029.
Cin: U22110DL1964PTC211907
Phone: +91 82877 98380/ +91 120-6251823
e-mail: mail@sterlingpublishers.in
www.sterlingpublishers.in

Drop by Drop: Nourished by every unfolding of life
© 2022, Nomita Kapur
ISBN 978 81 954046 7 4

Cover Design by
Sehej Kaur

All rights are reserved.
No part of this publication may be reproduced, stored in a retrieval system or transmitted, in any form or by any means, mechanical, photocopying, recording or otherwise, without prior written permission of the original publisher.

Printed in India

Printed and Published by Sterling Publishers Pvt. Ltd., Plot No. 13, Ecotech-III, Greater Noida - 201306, Uttar Pradesh, India

To my guru
Pandit Rajmani Tigunait
Thank you for showing me the way.

To my children
Karan *and* **Ananya**
There will surely be a time in your life when you will thread your own garland; until then, keep gathering the flowers.

But if the endlessly dead awakened a symbol in us,

perhaps they would evoke ... the raindrops

that fall onto the dark earth in springtime—

And we, who have always thought

of happiness as rising, would feel

the emotion that almost overwhelms us

whenever a happy thing falls.

Rainer Maria Rilke
Duino Elegies The 10th Elegy

Foreword

Drop by Drop is not a formal autobiography or a memoir but a song of life sung by someone who has lived fully. It is an expression of *kalyana mitra*, a benevolent friend's intention to share the best of herself. It is the author's *manasa puja* to the Lord of Life, who resides at the altar of everyone's heart.

Reflecting on her manuscript brought to mind the opening pages of *Living with the Himalayan Masters*, the classic work of my master, Swami Rama. There, as an offering to his master, he writes, "Who has, like thou, mingled the strains of joy and sorrow into the song of my life, enabling me to realize 'the joy that sits still on the lotus of pain and the joy that throws everything it has upon the dust and knows not a word'? . . . . Therefore, today the flower of undying gratitude offers its petals at thy lotus feet."

We are incomplete creations but we have the potential to become perfect. To awaken this potential, we have to recognize our strengths and weaknesses. This recognition largely depends on *vichara,* a well-understood and properly executed method of self-reflection and self-examination. With the help of vichara we can clearly see we are a combination of positive and negative tendencies. Love, compassion, kindness, forgiveness, fortitude and non-attachment, for example, are the positive and brighter aspects of our *samskaras*. Doubt, fear, anger, hatred, jealousy and greed are the dark aspects. These two sets of samskaras reside in us in an intermingled form. Through self-reflection and self-examination, we can assess their strengths and identify their trigger points. We can see the situations in which one of these tendencies awakens and dominates the others. Wisdom lies not as much in controlling those situations and circumstances as in cultivating a conscious awareness of the process of their awakening, and summoning our willpower to remain unperturbed.

Remaining unperturbed is not easy, but not impossible either. To maintain our equilibrium during disturbing moments, the scriptures prescribe *abhyasa* and *vairagya*. Making a sincere and conscious effort to remain focused on life's purpose is abhyasa. Protecting our mind from brooding on the past and entangling itself in anxiety pertaining to the future is vairagya.

Drop by Drop is an outcome of Nomita's self-reflection and ardent effort to practice abhyasa and vairagya. From this work it is clear she is not a hermit nor someone who can be crushed under the weight of worldly achievements. In these pages, Nomita shares her conviction that we are fortunate to be living in this wonderful world. Tussles and trials are not tragedies but doorways to understanding the mystery of divine will. As soon as we embrace the divine will happily and respectfully, enduring joy is ours. I hope and I pray that readers of this work find *their* enduring joy as they reflect on these uplifting anecdotes.

Pandit Rajmani Tigunait
Spiritual Head, Himalayan Institute

Preface

Drop by Drop is the fulfilment of a dream: a dream to know, and to find expression.

While my quest spanned over a decade, what has made it interesting is the vibrant mix of a modern education, an engaged family life, a professional life oriented towards deeper learning and a wide exposure through reading and travel.

All these facets of my life led me to recognize the underlying sameness in all our lives and the fact that while we have challenges, there is a joy in each of us that awaits room to express itself. My observations have been schooled and refined under the guidance of the teachers who have blessed my life. Studying Neuro-Linguistic Programming (NLP) in the UK under my teacher Sue Knight while exploring the wisdom of the Upanishads under various teachers in New Delhi, my deepest dive took me to the Himalayan Institute, Pennsylvania, USA, where true understanding emerged with the direct teachings of my spiritual master, Pandit Rajmani Tigunait.

This book is a distillation of what I have been taught and what I have come to know till now. Today, as I express myself, it is my honour to be able to contextualize ancient teachings in the modern context, something I have always aspired to do. It has also been a pleasure for me to see how my love for reading, music, food, fashion and travel – the delights of life – have found expression in my writings. For how else can life express itself and be experienced, if not through its touchstones?

The more I wrote, the greater was the catharsis. And as the book progressed, I found myself expressing more through poetry, for possibly, that is the true language of the heart.

Today, all I have in my heart is a prayer that we live our life in its fullest expanse and know it in its greatest depths.

Contents

Foreword   vii
Preface   ix
Introduction   xiii

ONE
Apurva
Coming into the Self

1.	The Blues	2
2.	What Do I Want?	6
3.	The Writing Table	11
4.	The Wisdom of Wine	16
5.	Apurva	20
6.	Alone	25

TWO
The Solitude of Strength
Knowing the Self

7.	The Meaning of Happiness	36
8.	Posture	44
9.	Hidden Revelation	51

10. The Solitude of Strength	59
11. Bead by Bead	65
12. Respectful	71
13. Clean and Dirty	78
14. Beyond Boundaries	83
15. Dewdrops of Forgiveness	88
16. Thanksgiving	93

THREE
Turnings of Joy
Abiding in the Self

17. A Meeting with Faith	100
18. The Wealth of Beauty	107
19. Turnings of Joy	113
20. The Calling of Love	119
21. Partnering with Death	129
22. Leaving My Legacy	136
Conclusion in continuation...	139
Acknowledgements	140
Bibliography	142
About the Author	143

Introduction

A wise person once told me 'the divine has no grandchildren', reinforcing the wisdom that we are all children of the divine. My family, friends and all those who have touched my life in a way to nurture me have been manifestations of the divine. My gratitude to them and to the great maternity that breathes over all our lives.

This book is about embracing life and, in turn, being in its embrace. It is about personal growth, the ground from which we begin to appreciate life and trust it to hold us.

Much of this book is about my personal unfoldment as I navigated my own life. I have lived a full yet ordinary life and with it came pain and joy as it does for all of us. The one thing that stood out for me was the pace and ferocity with which it unfolded, bringing with it a fair share of challenges. I spent many a year a bit taken aback by this unfolding, but life insisted on flowing its pace through me. It had its own design and its own direction. No matter how hard I tried, its tide was not for me to ebb.

It's true that growth comes at the edge of challenge and support. As the trumpets of challenge blew their horn, I found that the saints of support also came marching in. A decade of yearning and searching for answers landed me in the protection and nurturance of my spiritual teacher and a spiritual tradition. In my initial encounters with him, my teacher laid out the philosophy that has, since then, protected and nourished me. He pointed to the unity and auspiciousness of life and the inherent capacity of the mind. Enveloped in those words, I have embraced my life and all that unfolds as the grace of the divine. It has been my blessing to have life flow through me, and for me.

This collection of 22 essays is my endeavour to question and explore significant aspects of my life that emerged as compelling and warranted inner resolution. I neither wanted to negate them nor shy away from examining them. I chose to turn my gaze inwards, allowing my mind to access its own wisdom. There were no ready-made answers. Answers dawned as I explored the questions and began to hear and embody the messages that lay in their folds.

While the essays are independent of each other, they fall under three distinct moods, each mood deriving its flavour from feelings that resonated with me as I traversed my own journey.

How I navigated my life has been the only real choice I have made. Immersing myself in the unsettling polarities of life, I have endeavoured to understand them and find a context for them. This navigation has not been a magical, overnight effort. It has been a gradual journey of getting to know my humanity and my deeper truth, experiencing life, gaining insights, accepting gains and losses, and learning to love and let go.

I have been deeply grateful to observe the shift in myself as I began to touch my own essence and live the answers. It has largely been a transmutation of the old Self into the new, and letting that be the ground from which I now joyfully participate in the world.

As I inhabited this phase of deep introspection and transformation, I knew I wanted to share my reflections and learnings with others. I found myself penning my thoughts with a clarity and urgency I had never felt before. It was as though the journey of the last ten years of my life was finding its culmination and distilled expression. I had always known I would write a book, but now I found the book was writing itself through me.

While I understood the answers experientially, I also tested them through the wisdom contained in ancient Vedic scriptures of which I have been a keen and dedicated student. It has been my conscious endeavour to interlace the teachings and wisdom of some of these texts into my writings. Each essay contextualizes everyday life and stands as a testament to the age-old wisdom of these ancient texts of Indian philosophy.

As the challenges grow, our own expansion becomes an imperative and the only effectual antidote. Expansion, in turn, necessitates transformation. The challenges may be deeply personal or global, as COVID has recently shown us.

It is my hope that we may all allow ourselves to be devoted to the very process of life and grow through what life teaches, and have the trust and patience to allow the learnings to percolate, and be nourished – drop by drop.

ONE

Apurva

Coming into the Self

1

The Blues

The Blues, popularized by African-American artistes, is often described as a genre where singers express emotions rather than tell stories. It is the melody of intimate feelings – of loss and yearning, enveloped in a courageous voice. This compelling and unique style had a universal draw, and inspired many an artiste and their music. Elvis Presley sprang to fame singing 'Hound Dog' and dancing to 'Jailhouse Rock'. While he had his audience in raptures with his own style, a large part of his success lay in his appropriation of the longing, yearning and grit of the black artistes of the time.

I have to admit that I too have felt the 'blues' over the last several years. I remember, around the time I turned forty, I had numerous questions trafficking my mind – a restlessness I could not comprehend. I was seeking, searching, and yearning, not realizing the reason behind my unknowing.

As I approached fifty, someone asked me what crucial difference I saw in myself in the last decade. I was prompt to answer that while in my early forties I had many questions, in my early fifties I seem to have some answers. Maybe, as I pen down my thoughts today, all I am trying to do is make sense of my own journey. Let me share with you some lines I wrote more than a decade ago as a forty year-old, trying to make sense of life:

> One day she went running,
> Looking for something that was her reckoning,
> Frantically looking, holding on to time and its clocking.
> A restlessness abounds, a yearning so profound,
> Stirring of the soul, raising questions galore,
> A meaning to be found, an anchor to be dug in the ground.
> She asked, If I don't know why and where I am going,
> Hold my hand and take me to the showing.
> For I am life, and in my purpose, is my glowing.

Today as I read these lines, it is evident that I have had the blues and have felt them deeply. Yet, I am grateful that no matter how deep my blues were, they never turned into black. It intrigues me to realize that from the spectrum of colours that is VIBGYOR, the colour that never really reaches us is blue. As Rebecca Solnit points out, 'Light at the blue end of the spectrum does not travel the whole distance from the sun to us. It disperses among the molecules of the air, it scatters in water.' The beauty of the sky, the unattainability of the horizon, the depth of the ocean, are all nothing but the blue of this dispersion. The blue lies not so much in the dispersion as in the distance it draws attention to. For me, this distance is the yearning. Feeling the blues is feeling this gap; it's the longing to grasp the ungraspable. Possibly, in those very moments of restlessness, the far beckons nearness.

From another perspective, look at the blue of Lord Krishna. In the Indian subcontinent, Lord Krishna is the blue god, playing his games – his *leelas*. The spiritual traditions see blue as the colour of inclusiveness. By its very definition, what is all-inclusive is beyond boundary and division and thus beyond our grasp. Perhaps this is what makes blue ethereal. Lord Krishna the divine, dancing amongst humans, simultaneously being both.

Could the blues be both a yearning and an invitation? A beckoning by my soul, inviting me into its own ungraspable presence? Could it be an invitation for going beyond the known and firmly finding my space in the unknown? A process that seems to have its own momentum and own flowering? Is this the journey of the soul to find its divinity and humanity simultaneously?

This is possibly the journey beautifully and clearly captured by the *Mundaka Upanishad* and the story of the 'Two Birds':

> *dva suparna sayuja sakhaya samanam vrksam parisasvajate*
> *tayoranyah pippalam svadvattyanas'nannanyo abhicakasiti II*
> (*Mundaka*, 3.1.1)
>
> Two inseparable companions of fine plumage perch on the self-same tree.
>
> - One of the two feeds on the delicious fruit. The other, not tasting it, looks on.
> - The verse speaks of two birds who like good friends, are in fact one, and inseparable. Being one, they eat from the same tree. The Lower Bird is deeply engaged and is busy eating, while the other, the Higher Bird, is disengaged from all action and simply looks on.

- The two birds mentioned here are two aspects of the same reality. The enjoyer is the individual soul while the witness is pure consciousness. In our manifest form, we get engrossed in the dance of life and lose ourselves by identifying ourselves with our body–mind apparatus. Our attachments are sweet and bring us joy, while our aversions are bitter and bring us sorrow. In the bargain, we forget our true reality.
- Having lost ourselves, we yearn, we seek and search. Essentially, the Lower Bird has a kind of knowing of the Higher Bird and seeks to find and unite with it. It courageously covers a distance to unite with it.

The physical distance between the two birds is non-existent; they are the same, and they sit on the same tree – the body. Yet, the effort to unite warrants, as Joseph Campbell would say, a Hero's Journey – a breaking out of familiar strangeness.

We all yearn. We sense this yearning in ourselves and we sense it in other humans. Art, music, literature and poetry become expressions of it.

The blues, then, are a calling – possibly an invitation for us to take a journey unto ourselves. A call to risk getting lost and finding ourselves. Feeling the blues is a gift, a blessing, a transfiguration of a yearning into a journey that culminates in arrival. An invitation to life itself.

2

What Do I Want?

While going through one of my life's most significant crises, the most poignant and heartfelt advice I received was that it was now the right time for me to ask, 'what do I really want?'

I have found this one of the most challenging questions to answer. And interestingly, there was consensus amongst all my well-wishers that it is indeed a tough question to answer, but must be answered nevertheless.

As I began to search for the answer to this question, I did what most of us tend to do – I sought other people's views and advice. But I found that their advice kept shifting and did not always align with what I was feeling. I began to realize that the external world might not be the ultimate source for my answer.

One day, I was sitting at my optician's while he was prescribing new lenses for my worsening eyesight. We went through a few lenses of varying powers before we could arrive at the accurate one for me. Sitting there, the thought that came into perfect focus in my mind was that ultimately, the final choice was based on my verdict of what gave me the sharpest and most clear vision. The optometrist was merely facilitating the process and guiding me, and it was eventually my voice that prevailed.

Why do we often fail to have a voice or, even if we do, why do we fail to listen to it?

The story of the tenth man is very popular in the non-dualistic school of Indian philosophy and alludes to this failure.

> Ten men crossed a turbulent river. When they reached the other shore, one did a headcount and found only nine had crossed the river. They did this repeatedly with a different person counting each time, but the answer was always the same: nine. The reason the answer eluded them was because each time, the person doing the headcount forgot to count himself – he was the tenth man himself!

What amazes me about this story is how we forget to count ourselves in. No wonder we fail to listen to ourselves, and keep searching for answers in the external world.

For me, the point of inflection lay exactly here. Counting myself in, I now began to look for what I wanted and seek my answers in the depths of my inner being. Each time I wear my lenses, I am reminded that what guides me from the depth of my being is my inner-knowing itself.

Lord Krishna in the Bhagavad Gita points his student Arjuna towards this:

> *Uddhared atmanatmanam natmanam avasadayet*
> *Atmaiva hyatmano bandhur atmaiva ripur atmanah II*
>
> (BG, 6.5)
>
> One should cause the deliverance of the Self by the Self. Self alone is the kinsman of the Self, but can be the enemy too.
>
> - Given our deep-rooted habits of being externally oriented, we search for answers outside ourselves. But when we get into our inner world, we realize that what we are seeking outside is actually within.
> - We are fully equipped and have all the means to attain the truth. In asking 'what I want' what I am seeking is the 'I' itself. The Self looks for the Self and the Self is attained by the Self alone.

While I continued to digest Lord Krishna's teachings, I stayed with my question. Asking this question put me into many places at the same time. I wonder if what I want today is different from what I wanted yesterday, and whether it will be what I will want in the future.

When I ask myself what I want, my thought process tends to lean against what I know, and what I have heard. But both these are benchmarked against the past. I know what I know today largely because of the past. But is the past going to give me the solution I need for the present? The notion that the past influences the present rests on the understanding of cause and effect and the classic linearity of that relationship. Look at the batsman tackling the ball that was bowled to him. We could say that the ball was hit by the bat. But looking again, what about the motivation of the batsman to hit the ball, what about his judgement on the spin of the ball? Was the spin of the ball itself not a function of the motivation and skill of the bowler? In the way this ball was tackled by the batsman, will it affect the way the next ball will be bowled? It begins to appear that separate events don't really exist, and that all events seem to form a continuum wherein cause and effect merge. My judgement of what I want is, at best, an approximation of the past, and so will remain a poor one at that.

Coming back to the main question: What do I want? What I want is probably a hypothesis of the future. At best a hypothesis, because by the time the future arrives, it is already the present. Look at the clock: the future is a second after the present – the present itself being a second which passes even before we blink. Can my thinking negotiate this speed? This seems to be the real challenge. The answer is not forthcoming, and it all seems like a snake trying to eat its tail.

The knife of intellect has very sharp edges. Yet, the more I slice to find the answer to what I want, the fuzzier the question itself becomes. In the blurry edges of the question, several others now begin to arise:

- Is what I want the same as what I need?
- If I were to have what I feel I need, would I still really want it?
- Is it true that I don't have what I want?
- Or have I, in any way, blocked it?
- Am I ready to deal with the way I block what I want?

The very process of questioning was making me begin to touch something palpable but indescribable. There was a time when the atom was considered to be the tiniest segment of reality. Today we know otherwise. Scientists agree that as we keep segmenting reality into parts, after a point, segmentation itself begins to reveal wholeness – a palpable and indescribable reality.

This capacity to slice, acknowledging the parts and yet seeing the underlying wholeness, is a gift of the inquiry itself. Asking the question 'what do I want?' and allowing the answer to emerge, may require us to go into a space which is beyond thought, speech and action. This may be the space of inner knowing – the very ground where the answer will greet its own question.

But perhaps the ground needs tilling before it can become fertile. I reckon this was the truth that Rainer Maria Rilke was alluding to when he advised his young protégé to '… go through your development quietly and seriously; you cannot disrupt it more by looking outwards and expecting answers from without to questions that only your innermost instinct in your quietest moments will perhaps be able to answer'.

At this point, the best I can do is to resolutely look inwards. As I continue to inquire into what I want, I begin to get glimpses of what I am. Yet I know that before I can put my glimpses into words and action, a certain clarity and firm landing is required. Until then, accepting the advice of Rilke, I choose to 'live the question for now' and perhaps then I will gradually 'live my way into the answer' as well.

3

The Writing Table

We human beings, inherently, are collectors. We collect objects, power, status, money and memories amongst many other things. In my life, something I seem to have visibly collected are writing tables. Collecting them was never my aspiration but they seem to have housed themselves comfortably around me.

It began thirty years ago – dreams of having a study, in which there would be a big writing table where I would sit and write.

But many things must happen before a dream comes true. I journeyed through higher studies, a profession, marriage, children, a busy home and an even busier life, before I came to a point where I placed my first writing table in a newly curated study. My pride and joy. But soon I felt trespassed by the household traffic that wanted to go through my study to reach the connecting gym.

Feeling slightly ousted, I decided to invest in a new study table to be placed in my bedroom with the firm resolve to anchor myself there and write. But I suppose a reflective space and a spouse are mutually exclusive.

Still yearning for that space and refusing to forsake my dream, I decided to invest in yet another table to be placed in a newly rented apartment my mother was taking up in the neighbourhood. A definite third table, which I knew was going to initiate me into my writing career. A terrible fall and hip fracture later, I soon found my mother and the table juxtapositioning themselves in my home.

Looking around with some curiosity, I found that my home had more writing tables than the number of rooms and yet, somehow, I had not managed to sit at any one of them to write!

So where had I been? Had I been writing or only collecting and placing writing tables? To be honest, I had sneaked out and furiously written in parking lots, elevators, and even recorded my voice while walking and driving. Writing had not been about putting pen to paper on a writing table, but it had been about a flow of thoughts – and the venue, the location and the medium became less and less relevant.

Today, the trajectory of my life has changed yet again. As an empty nester, I sweep through the different rooms of my home and sit at each of my writing tables in rotation. I place myself differently at the different tables and begin to write. A flow of thoughts coalesces into words, which manifest on paper as an arrangement of letters.

Who is really writing? My thoughts flow and my hands type. Words appear and meanings unfold. But when I pull back the thread, I recognize that it's a flow that began from somewhere deeper than my mind, and then flows through my mind, working its way through my hands and showing up as words. The writing table pales in significance. The more I do this, the more varied my thoughts and writing become, and yet something begins to strike me as constant.

Am I the table? Am I the hand? Am I the words? Am I the mind? Who am I?

Who was it who was enlivening the mind, allowing the thoughts to emerge, and finding their expression on paper? At this point, the fallacy of René Descartes' claim of 'I think therefore I am' started to become apparent. Just as notes of music arise from and dissolve in silence, thoughts arise from and dissolve in a certain ground. That ground was inviting attention.

As we look beyond the branch to see the moon, I began to look beyond the table, the words and the thoughts, to look at the spring well. Whichever table I wrote on, would my words change? Whether I typed or wrote with ink on paper, would my alphabets change? Whether I wrote my words in English or Hindi, would my thought change? And yet, if all my tables, inks, words and thoughts changed, what would never change? Sitting at each of my tables, I began to notice each of my hues and yet recognized the seeming source from which they all sprang. It had been 'me' all along. Parked between the parking lot and various writing tables, it was 'I' that had my own still momentum all along.

I was the source, and had always been. I began to see that my mind, my thoughts, my words and my tables were all housed in me. I was not housed in them. Many things must happen before a dream is fulfilled. The dream, and all ensuing effort, both stem from me. What must happen must happen first in me. Each time I sat at my various tables, I sat with a growing recognition of who sits. I, not so much a body but as a presence, sit at my table.

I began to find resonance in the wisdom of the *Kathopanishad* which says:

> *Yena rupam ghandam sabdan sparssams ca maithunam*
> *Etenaiva vijanati, kim atra parisiayate; etad vai tat II*
> (*Katho*, 2:1:3)
>
> What is atman? That which is not the object that is seen, but That which sees the object. Who perceives form, taste, smell, sound and touch.
>
> - I taste a dish, but who is tasting? Not the tongue, because it is also an object. There is an awareness guiding the tongue itself.
> - The same awareness guides and witnesses the mind during waking and dreaming. In deep sleep, my mind is at rest and yet I exist.
> - At the deepest level, I exist as consciousness.

Beyond the physicality of the writing tables I recognize my own intangible presence. And yet, as I sit, I thank my stars that while the spirit lies within me, I am not a ghost. Alas, what would a spirit be if it had no mind, hands nor tables to express itself? A wandering spirit with no ground to touch. The foot would never know itself till it touches the ground. I would never know myself till I touch the manifest. And yet I recognize myself only by interacting with that which I am not.

Today I recognize my unqualified presence and the fact that there is a relationship between me, my thoughts, my words, my writing, and my writing tables. I can't think myself into existence. I exist; therefore, I think, and so I write. It is my existence that finds expression in my own thoughts and words spelt out over my collection of writing tables.

Slowly I see all my tables merge and what I am left with is an experience – a relationship. More than being collectors we are, inherently, composite beings, and what we collect is merely an extended expression of our own Self.

4

The Wisdom of Wine

At the outset, let me admit that I enjoy wine – its various bodies, blends and colours. The romance around it is enduring too. Evenings spent with friends, dim lighting, music, laughter, food and wine make up some of my most cherished memories.

Wine just has a way of drawing you in, sometimes to the point where consumption exceeds resolve. This has happened to me on occasion, and one such time became a moment of reckoning. I am not talking of hangovers and acidity attacks, which seem easy to deal with. What I am talking about is a 'wine blackout'. My inability to recall parts of the evening astounded me. It's not just that I couldn't recall what had happened – it was like the event never happened at all, and so no memory of it was formed. Yet, I would find snatches of what I had said in my memory. Was it a wine-induced blackout or a 'brownout'? Either way, I began to recognize that somewhere my mind had been hijacked.

I seem to have said things that I probably meant but would have never said in as many words and in that manner if I had been more in possession of my conscious mind. The first layers of questions that sprang up were: What do I feel at an unconscious level that I don't recognize at the conscious level? Interestingly, it was in those very moments that I had a glimpse of how two unrelated parts of me coexist.

The next level of questions that began to arise for me were: Who is the 'me' that spoke those words? Which 'me' went to bed and somehow slept amidst high-traffic dreams? Who was the 'me' who woke up the next morning knowing that what had happened had been avoidable? Who am I? How do I recognize myself? The alcohol-consuming human side of me was being questioned by a deeper Self that wanted to be known and heard.

What was becoming obvious to me was that there was a deeper Self, which was somewhat hidden behind the recesses of the mind. Bypassing the mind was creating a space for me to access this true Self. But then again, I wonder, if not the mind, which is the instrument that would allow me to know myself? Explorations of the Self bring me to two questions: What is the relationship between the mind and the Self – are the mind and the Self the same or different? Does the Self get kidnapped by the mind?

Looking for answers, I delved into Vedic scriptures. Their blessings unfolded as answers.

The *Ashtavakra Gita*, a profound text of the highest calibre, throws clear light on the first question as it distinguishes the mind from the real Self:

> *ragadvesau manodharmau na manaste kadacana*
> *nirvikalpo'si bodhatma nirvikarah sukham cara II*
>
> *(AVG, 15:5)*
>
> Desire and anger are objects of the mind, but the mind is
> not yours (not of the Self) nor has it ever been. The Self
> is choice-less; it is awareness itself, and it is
> unchanging – so we should live happily.

The corollary to this is that the mind is ever-changing. What changed that night was the mind as it went through its different layers. In fact, it was my mind that spoke, slept and felt remorse in its different modifications. The Self remained, unchanging and ever-present.

It's clear that the mind and the Self are distinct from one another. Yet, what must their relationship be? What was my Self trying to do that night? It was definitely trying to show up and make its presence felt! How could it possibly express itself? Can it – and does it – express itself through the mind?

Isn't the mind a conduit to allow the Self to express itself in our world?

If the mind is the conduit for the expression of the Self, then how can it do a good job if it is busy playing truant and is entangled in its own modifications, confusions and delusions?

Why does the morning after a night of heavy drinking feel so low? As the mind gets hijacked, what ensues is an absence of being. This felt loss is real and viscerally experienced. The discomfort wanes only when the mind has regained clarity and the Self resumes expressing itself through the mind.

I am in awe as I begin to comprehend that the mind's power to be a good conduit comes from the Self itself! The mind empowered by the Self is the instrument that takes us back to the Self.

Would it not then become an imperative for us to reclaim the luminosity, clarity and calmness of our minds? If we don't, do we run the risk of forsaking the Self?

Patanjali's *Yoga Sutra* boldly answers in the affirmative:

> *Vrtti sarupyam itaratra II*
>
> (*YS*, 1:4)
>
> Elsewhere the Self conforms to the *vrittis*, the roaming tendencies, of the mind.
>
> - The mind defines truth in light of its subtle impressions.
> - We then use all our resources to find truth or the Self as we have defined it.
> - Our comprehension of our true Self stretches only as far as our mind. Sadly, our mind, tainted with its afflictions, reflects a tainted version of the Self. Intermingled with the mind, the Self stands forsaken.
> - But we forget that the Self is independent of the mind and is in fact the *adhaar* – the source – of the mind itself. How can it ever be defined by the mind?

That night was a time of a 'blackout of the mind'. But then the light of the Self propelled me to ponder and look for resolution.

All resolutions ultimately lie in the Self. A clear mind gets us there. My gratitude for the wisdom of wine – a call for the clarity of mind.

5

Apurva

It is 1st January today. It is a good time to make resolutions for the new year, especially as a horrifying COVID-infested year concludes. But what intrigues me about resolutions is that however enthusiastically we make them, we do so mostly to break them.

So, let's look at the moment of reckoning, when the clock strikes midnight. Saying goodbye to the year gone by is an attempt to bid farewell to the old and look forward to the new. We naturally wish for new experiences, aspirations and realities. Unfortunately, we do so with an 'old mind'.

Welcoming the new year as the clock struck 12, I wondered, if we were gifted a 'new mind' instead, would we still feel the need to make resolutions? So, as the new year dawns, my resolve is for a 'new mind' rather than new happenings to keep rebooting the old mind. In the eastern traditions of philosophy, this is called *apurva* – newness. It is a freshness that embraces our life where nothing changes yet everything stands changed – a new reality stands before us, which is a gift of the 'new mind'.

Let me explain this further with a verse from the *Brihadranyaka Upanishad*:

> *...sa yathakamo bhavanti tatkraturbhavati, yatkraturbhavati tatkarma kurute, yatkarma kurute tat abhisampadyate II*
> (*Bh*, 4:4:5)
>
> You are what your deep, driving desire is. As your desire is, so is your will. As your will is, so is your deed. As your deed is, so is your destiny.
>
> - This highlights a triad of desire–will–destiny. As a desire awakens and I keep thinking about it, I strengthen my desire and it becomes will. Will has the power to make us act, and action, in turn, produces results. Through our will we can create our destiny and fulfil our desires.

But herein lie the difficulties we encounter with our resolutions.

Despite my desire to lose weight and resolving to go on a diet each new year, I fail to do so. Why?

I want to be a successful professional in life and yet despite my potential and talent, why don't I make a go of it?

Exploring these questions brings us to a hidden and missing dimension – thought.

> So, the relationship looks somewhat like this: ***desire-will-thought and action-destiny***

Thus, while I may aspire to be a successful professional, fear of failure or minimizing myself through self-limiting thought patterns may keep incapacitating me. And yet, ironically, I do achieve my deepest desire. Fear stems from a desire for safety, and in sacrificing my desire for success, I honour my deepest desire – for safety.

Eastern philosophy explains the above as *sankalpa* and *vikalpa*. Sankalpa is my resolve to move towards a certain outcome; but what may impede the process is a counter-thought, vikalpa.

Let me elaborate by borrowing from 'The Four Desires' by Rod Stryker, an eminent yoga and meditation teacher.

> **Kalpa** = the rule or assumption we follow above all others
>
> **Sankalpa** = the rule or assumption that takes us closer to our higher Self/Self-actualization
>
> **Vikalpa** = vi + kalpa = the rule or assumption that separates, takes apart or pulls us back

Thus, vikalpas are those thoughts – beliefs and mental constructs – that separate us from our highest Self and from the destiny our soul is seeking to fulfil. While we believe that our resolve is resolute, it is actually weakened by the onslaught of our own vikalpa. Much emphasis is placed on strengthening our determination and willpower, but what we fail to realize is the disastrous effects of not knowing our vikalpas and leaving them unresolved. Fulfilling our dreams means assuaging our vikalpas.

While sankalpas are our conscious resolve, vikalpas are like our unconscious and counter resolve, moving us away from our destiny. Caught between this tussle of sankalpa and vikalpa, gaps between aspirations and achievements create stress.

While performance is the external indicator, the more important thing is to notice the internal dynamics. Neuroscience widely accepts that when we undergo chronic stress, regions of the brain associated with executive decision-making and goal-directed behaviour become atrophied. And at the same time, sectors of the brain linked to habit formation grow as a result of stress. Over a period of time, this vicious cycle becomes a cause for impaired decision-making and atrophied dynamism. We come to inhabit this trap and live with a gnawing sense of being mired down.

Each thought wave influences the mind and therein affects destiny. Our unconscious mind, through its vikalpas, yields its power over our conscious mind and holds us hostage. For any personal growth and outward achievement, the battle between our conscious desires and our unconscious tendencies must be won by the conscious mind enlisting the unconscious in the fulfilment of our resolve.

Recognizing how much or how little we actually strive to achieve our resolve is a definite clue to vikalpa. Herein lies the space of unfulfilled dreams. Thomas Merton, a Christian monk, pointed out that all answers to our identity lie in the gap between 'what I am living for' and 'what is keeping me from living fully for the thing I want to live for'.

Our sankalpas and vikalpas each have a language of their own. We set our sankalpas and resolutions in words because words are the language of the conscious mind. This empowers the conscious mind and so propels our resolve. The language of the unconscious mind is not words, but feelings and images. As long as we remain victims of past hurts, fear, anger, greed, jealousy and confusion, we will continue to have a negative mind, reflected in feelings coming from our unconscious, our vikalpas. They not only block and weaken our sankalpa, but also push us into dark spaces in life. Thus, repeating our sankalpa does not strengthen our resolve as much as letting go of the vikalpa does.

Our feelings and images become the clue to our unconscious patterns and unresolved issues, and are also the doorways for reset. Soliciting the unconscious and aligning it with our conscious intentions is knowing how to make the unconscious and conscious intentions symbiotic. Otherwise, we are left simply parroting our resolves, which becomes a tedious exercise in patience.

Protection comes our way from the fact that our brain is elastic; it can restore itself and its functioning as well as rewire itself. The current concept of neuroplasticity sheds light on creating new thought patterns through which the mind can be rewired, and new grooves formed. It's plain to see that creating a new mind is not just about deleting the old mind; it is an active process of rewiring the mind through a structured and organized approach. Many spiritual and mindfulness practices can lead us there. The active practice of meditation, breathing, knowledge and contemplation can embed the new patterns so deeply in our minds that they become a way of living and thinking.

Human aspiration never ceases to live out its fullest potential as we journey through life. Our mastery over our vikalpas has more to do with our own ripening over time. To recognize them is to be open to our own revelation of our deepest truth. They carry the marks of our inner struggle and gift us with an earned understanding of our own potential. They instruct us towards our own completeness. As I consciously frame my aspirations for the new year, let my 'new mind' take me to my destiny. May this year be the Year of Apurva – my new mind – and may all resolves be fulfilled through this newness.

6

Alone

Three decades of a busy householder's life were coming to an end. I stood looking over an empty nest. All the members of what I had come to know as my immediate family were moving on and moving out, while I stood in the very same spot. The foundation of my identity itself as I had lived it so far, was shifting.

The dread of loneliness is something that plagues us all at different times in our lives. For me, this was my moment of reckoning. Life as I had known it was changing right before my eyes. The comfort and solidity of what I had come to know as my ground was quivering and imploding right before my eyes. I stood with a clear realization that now I was on my own and I had to prepare for an independent life.

Loneliness

Loneliness was my first encounter with being alone, and I experienced it as grief, loss and insecurity. It was like solitary confinement. A prison where I felt trapped, looking out at what had been my world and wanting it to continue to envelop me. The pain of loneliness is visceral, held as a tightness in the muscles that fail to relax and a heart that beats to its anxiety.

It is a space one comes to inhabit and in doing so, recognizes the void.

It's strange how we come to define life. We define it based on people, geography, events, routines and rituals, amongst others. Life is a composite of who we are, whom we are with, where we locate ourselves, and when and what we see and do. Languishing in disillusionment, I began to examine my own definitions. The more I played with the definitions, the more I realized it was not the definitions that were defining me and my actions. It was the meaning and value I had placed on my various roles that allowed for the definition to cement in the first place. The more loosely I began holding my definitions, the more I began to see beyond the structures of those definitions.

In eastern traditions of spiritual life, four stages of life have been laid out: *Brahmacharya* (student), *Grihastha* (householder), *Vanaprastha* (retiring to the forest) and *Sannyasa* (renunciate). Through my spiritual journey, I had understood that we transition between these stages and must prepare ourselves for them. What came as a surprise was that maybe these stages come calling on us even before we realize it. At the age of 51, was I to prepare myself for forest life? It seemed I didn't have to leave for the forest as the forest had come to me.

Vanaprastha is about training oneself to let go of attachments and preparing for a solitary life. In the modern world as we know it, it seems we are being relieved of this effort. We don't have to prepare to let go of our attachments as the objects of our attachment themselves seem to leave. Even the vocabulary of our world is changing. We have transitioned from 'virtual reality' to 'augmented reality' or 'AR' to 'erasAR technology', software that appears to remove objects from the landscape to allow for an altered experience. Life as an independent person and an empty nester was my vanaprastha coming to me. It was the erasAR technology at work in my life.

Consolation

As objects are removed from the landscape, what springs up first and foremost is space. A space in which certain things recede in their visibility while others emerge in sharpness and clarity. A consolation of sorts:

> From time to time
> The clouds give rest
> To the moon beholders
> (Basho, in a haiku)

As the walls of my home are swept away, I begin to see the sun. Osho had said, 'Let it all go. See what stays.' Seeing was an art that I was having to cultivate anew.

Hemmingway was right in pointing out that 'the dignity of movement of an iceberg is due to only one-eighth of it being above water'. I began to make an effort to see what lay in the unseen layers of my life.

I looked in the mirror not to look at myself but to look for myself. It took courage to ask difficult questions in a situation which was already difficult. But when the pain became unbearable, the only relief was the gap between each spasm. It is in these gaps that hope takes shape, moulded by courageous questions. The questions are not the answers, but they allow for much to be seen and revisited.

The gift of loneliness was turning out to be a kind of inhabited awakening. It was giving me the courage to heed questions arising from an inner voice. A motivator of sorts, moving me towards accepting and recalibrating.

Being Lost

With my reference points being taken away, I experienced a sense of being lost. I wasn't sure which disappeared first – the objects or my world? But I could feel them both fade.

Many unknowns can be calculated as long as there is a relational equation between at least two known quantities and we are clear about some assumptions. This is the assertion of mathematics. But is this true of life too?

My life was calling on me to calculate with only the unknowns. As my home emptied and the grip of COVID tightened with unfathomable ferocity, stringent lockdowns and home isolations made my life all but solitary. Feeling locked in and locked up, I felt like I had no world to connect to. I needed a world and I needed to reconfigure myself within its knowns. This was to be my journey. I realized somewhere I was making a transition from knowing to not-knowing and from certainties to probabilities. The very vocabulary of navigation needed renewal.

The blessing of getting lost is that we emerge on the other side of the unknown with better knowing. I have often seen my dog recovering from hurt and discomfort. He withdraws, curls up and licks his wound till he is feeling better. I knew this pause, this withdrawal, was going to be crucial for my recovery too. Refraining from going out and indulging in instruments of forgetfulness, I chose to nest at home.

Grounding myself in the mundane was at once comforting and energizing. Laying down my busyness and allowing for a space of nothingness to emerge was the gift of recovery I was giving myself.

Could I be lost in one world but manage to find myself in another? I began to feel that the 'lost-ness' is a need for human presence to be reconfigured. Can being lost be a gift? Unless we realize this, being lost is a curse – an unconscious and helpless state. I was coming to accept that being lost was the only way in which I could then find myself, anew. It seemed that life was prompting me to live it as a question rather than a carefully constructed statement.

A song I heard a lot in those days was 'I Hope You Dance' by Lee Ann Womack. The line that resonated with me most was 'I hope you still feel small when you stand beside the ocean.' Was this the new vocabulary I was looking for? This is unlike our everyday vocabulary which expresses our location. For example, I am standing with the ocean to my left, but then the same ocean stands to my right as I turn around. Herein lies the absurdity of trying to locate, myself with myself as the reference point. Taking a cue from Lee Ann's song, I wondered if I could locate myself better with reference to the ocean? No matter which way I turn, I will still stand west of the ocean if that is where the ocean is located. Maybe the language of navigation is one of surrender to the larger, the unmoving, the constant.

Being lost was about relocating myself and establishing a relational equation between a constant and myself, the variable. What was that constant going to be? I was looking for my North Star – ever bright and constant.

Immersion

The Unseen and the Hidden

Being lost was becoming about mastering the art of immersion in lost-ness itself. Now, it was not only about being lost but also about losing the definition of myself as I knew it and remembered it. The continuity of memory itself was becoming a weak measure of myself. Stripped of my identity as a householder, there was no point holding on to that memory. I couldn't possibly define my present based on the past. For a while, it was a relief to remain hidden.

But could I remain hidden endlessly? Hiding is a conscious act. In the game of hide-and-seek, we hide consciously. It gives us a sense of excitement and power. While hiding can be a thrill, the thrill vanishes into deep disappointment when the hidden begs to be found. The same is true in real life too. Hiding my ideas, beliefs, emotional ties as well as my convictions may have served the cause of a mistaken sense of self-preservation. But it was becoming evident that in remaining hidden from myself, I could cause my own destruction – because, remember, seven layers of an iceberg do lie hidden.

The unseen is not the same as the hidden. While the hidden is marked by absence, the unseen is marked by presence. The unseen has autonomy, identity and a presence of its own. It's like the unquestionable presence of the unseen mother for a child. Being alone was choosing to be hidden and lost, and in being so, coming to know myself in my own unseen presence. Sometimes, the loss is the gain.

Relocation

So much human endeavour lies in the unseen. The past was losing its charm and the future, its excitement. The only choice I had was to see the present, and what it held. A kind of silence was descending. As all stories were seeming to stop, I was being silent and also becoming the silence.

When the inner quest takes urgency, the first thing that stops is all external-oriented activities, which work as wonderful distractions, but keep us stuck in the very same state. Art, music and other forms of creative self-expression begin to take centre stage in these moments of our life. I, too, listened to music and poetry, but I began to realize that these were not my creative expressions. At best, they were helping me locate my inner feelings but were offering me scant tools to manage them.

What held my hand and supported me, was dedicated practice and dispassion. There couldn't have been a better time to test all that I had been studying over the years. It seemed that I had been orienting myself towards the time-tested tools of *abhyasa* (practice) and *vairagya* (dispassion) as detailed by Sage Patanjali in the *Yoga Sutra*, only to prepare for this time in my life:

> *abhyasavairagyabhyam tannirodhah II*
>
> (*YS*, 1:12)
>
> That [roaming tendency of the mind] can be controlled through practice and non-attachment.
>
> - According to Patanjali, abhyasa means making an ardent effort to retain an inward flow of the mind while vairagya is cultivating a mind free from the colourings of deeply embedded mental impressions.

It is true that the map is not the territory. So how can I know the territory? The journey begins with calming inner unrest and thus paving the path to knowing the territory.

My immersion was guided by this twofold system of yoga of which I have been a student. Abhyasa allowed me to build my mind's capacity to flow peacefully, while vairagya allowed my mind to be free of its own sufferings.

The foundation of abhyasa lies in this: recognizing that alignment allows for stillness, and stillness sustains joy. I established a firm daily practice of yoga postures and meditation. As I would lie on my yoga mat and feel the floor hold my body, I would feel even more the space that my body occupies. I was beginning to locate myself in my own personal space. As my mind aligned with my breath, I found stillness. I began to rest in a sense of peace that was springing from deep within.

Vairagya or dispassion, which is so often misunderstood as renunciation, was the ground on which I was beginning to rid myself of hidden mental habits. Guided by my teacher, I began to understand that to live in this world with dispassion was to free oneself of one's own mental trappings. With sustained self-reflection, standing on this ground of freedom, I could see how, many a time, I had been in my own self-imposed exile.

As my twofold practice deepened, there was a certain calm that I had begun to carry, along with a greater ability to hear the sounds of my own silence.

In the silence, I truly began to appreciate the verse from the Bhagavad Gita that my spiritual teacher had pointed me towards, in helping me grow through this phase:

> *dva imau purushau loke ksharash chakshara eva cha*
> *ksharah sarvani bhutani kuta-stho 'kshara uchyate II*
>
> (*BG*, 15:16)
>
> There are two kinds of being in creation, the *kshar* (perishable) and the *akshar* (imperishable). The perishable are all beings in the material realm while the absolute is said to be imperishable.
>
> - The body, breath, senses and conscious mind are the gross units of life and are said to be perishable as they undergo constant change.
> - The supreme Self is the ultimate eternal reality. With the realization of the supreme Self, the individual self becomes one with the supreme Self.

In my world, I was experiencing two realities. One was constantly changing and the other, unseen, was unchanging and constant. On the one hand, I stood watching the landscape of my ever-changing external world and on the other, I stood recognizing the unchanging 'I' within which all these experiences were unfolding.

I am not sure when I will know the 'absolute' in totality, but in my daily practices and moments of contemplation, I knew I had glimpses of the eternal. A journey from the excitement of the gross, to the joy of the subtle.

Together

As the gaze of others waned in my life, I had no choice but to deepen my own inward gaze. This has been my greatest gift.

In doing so, I regained my own power and my own agency. I allowed the responsibility of being the author of my own life to flow through me. At the same time, my internal coherence and congruity gifted me with acceptance. It allowed me to experience my sufferings and my joys in an embodied way.

In my aloneness, as I navigated my way through my lostness, I gathered a sense of membership: to myself and others. I released the hold I was keeping on my identity as I realized it was as futile as trying to hold a fistful of sand. And now, I have begun to see others with the same soft gaze.

The time when I felt I had lost everything, is when I found myself. The 'alone' in me is a space that allows me to heal and then brings me back to life. A space laden with the gift of inner anchorage, where dissipation allows for a more gathered self.

Today, for me, being alone is living my blessings and is not a state of condemnation. As my tears soften the hardened cracks of my heart, I find myself joyfully standing 'together alone'.

TWO

The Solitude of Strength

Knowing the Self

7

The Meaning of Happiness

D.H. Lawrence had once said, 'Tragedy ought to be a great kick at misery.' Nothing rings truer than this in today's COVID-struck world. Sitting amidst the ravages of the disease and listening to news of loss in families, I begin to wonder about the life we were leading just prior to the outbreak of the pandemic. We were talking gallantly about human will and achievements, trade and commerce, digital prowess, efficiency and effectiveness, the shrinking of the world as we conquered it. We felt entitled and rewarded ourselves with possessions and experiences. A deluge of spending and self-gratification became the symbol of human achievement. What unwittingly came to be seen as the 'pursuit of happiness' actually saw a decline in happiness and character in many. Maybe the COVID tragedy stands as a kick to the misery of the futile pursuit of happiness.

But today, amidst this morbid environment, what shall happiness be? Health, safety, well-being and the fortune of having the family intact seem now to be the goals worth pursuing. The enigma of happiness continues to baffle! Maybe Rousseau was right when he hypothesized that wealth does not involve having many things, but rather, having what we long for. And maybe herein lies the insurmountable task of achieving happiness.

With the pursuit of happiness as the declaration of our time, the world seems to have seen a degeneration of sorts. Our desires became wants and our wants became our needs. Needless to say, political ambition and economic power ably supported by the media, advertising and the technological revolution rendered us privileged, entitled and yet somewhat harried.

The psychological manoeuvring in our generation has had a significant role to play. The onslaught of motivational speakers spreading the message of 'you can control your life' tried to bring happiness down to the famous '10 rules', as if these 10 rules were the distillation of all the wisdom mankind needed. Even today, when digital media pops up talk of '10 ways to improve your XYZ', what is implicit in the tagline is that as things stand, you fall short. Cinema and magazines glorified wealth and luxury. What crept into society was a sense of deprivation and envy. The world of advertising began to thrive when it shifted focus from the attributes of the product to the person who would possess the product and what competitive advantage he stood to gain. For example, the Patek Philippe watch was not so much about its attributes but about being a legacy – the attribution was to the buyer of the watch.

As growth curves pointed upwards and the world heralded the seasons of plenty, what began to grow exponentially was that sense of deprivation. Caught between chasing dreams, demanding equal opportunity and the belief that we are the masters of our destiny, the pursuit of happiness continued. Plotted on a graph it may look like an asymptotic curve – proximal to the target yet never reaching it.

The history of Romanticism added another burden: that of the perfect love relationship. The entire burden of our happiness fell on a few people who were seen to be custodians of our happiness. The spouse and the family began to shoulder this burden. But as happiness expert Dan Gilbert puts it, only a happy person can be 'happier' in and through his relationships.

Sociology has already thrown a lot of light on the fact that 'it takes a village to raise a child'. It is true that it takes a large family or tribal support system to raise a child. Yet, what does it mean to raise a child? Is the act of rearing just one of ensuring the child's survival or is it about ensuring all of the child's developmental needs – physical, mental and emotional? Only a child whose developmental needs have been met will be a happy child. As communities disintegrate and families move towards being nuclear, it becomes effortful to raise a happy child.

While these have been the footprints of history, Dan Gilbert begs our attention to look at another reality. Interestingly, he points out this: if you observe two people, one who loses a leg and another who wins a lottery, then a year from the event, both are equal in their happiness levels. The reason? Maybe that non-conscious thought processes allow humans to change their view of the world such that they feel better about the world they are in. Our longings and worries are overrated because we have it in us to manufacture the very commodity we are chasing. Therein lies our ability to make peace with what we have and, in turn, generate our own happiness.

This, in fact, is a crucial capacity we humans have but are blind to. Maybe this is what lies behind the adage 'time is the best healer'. Is time the healer or is it our innate capacity to find happiness? And could our ability to be happy be linked to avoiding the mistake of overrating the differences between future events and choices, and finding acceptance with the present?

Adam Smith, the father of Economics, seems to have had this insight. It seems the whole engine of economics runs on the fact that it cognizes this capacity of humans and yet mocks the fact that we are blind to our own capacity. This blindness seems to keep the engine of growth greased.

> ... the source of both the misery and disorder of human life, seems to arise from over-rating the difference between one permanent situation and another. Some of these situations may, no doubt deserve to be preferred to others: but none of them can deserve to be pursued with that passionate ardor which drives us to violate the rules either of prudence or of justice, or to corrupt the future tranquility of our minds either by shame from the remembrance of our own folly, or by remorse from the horror of our own injustice.

(Adam Smith, *The Theory of Moral Sentiments*)

It would be rather futile if, as sentient beings, we grasped our condition better but still failed to overcome it. When all doors shut, we have no option but to turn inwards. Today, in an era of prolonged lockdowns when most avenues of external gratification are unavailable, what is to become of our quest for happiness? What can possibly calm unending human anguish? In and through the pandemic, maybe the task at hand is to renew our perspectives. Maybe the task is to understand the 'meaning of happiness' rather than engage in the futile 'pursuit of happiness'.

The Meaning of Happiness

Let our happiness not be a superhuman task, for, in the words of Camus, 'superhuman is the term for tasks we take a long time to accomplish, that's all'. Maybe the journey of happiness is simpler and imminently achievable.

Maybe it is about switching out of the misery that ensues from expecting to be and achieve even more: the '–er' – greater, smarter, wealthier, thinner – and freeing ourselves from solidifying into '–isms' – capitalism, communism, perfectionism, even veganism. The need for the '–er' and the '-ism' comes from a rejection of the ordinary in favour of the extraordinary. This spins us into the cycle of desire and ambition. A true meaning of happiness could be setting free our unhappiness from the clutches of desire and ambition such that it may morph into contentment and peace. For else, how would we find our way out of Dante's nine circles of hell and unhappiness?

At the end of the day, when death comes calling, how little does what we pursue really matter? The more we achieve earthly pleasures, the more we realize how hollow they make us. In turn, can we be content with who we are? Could it be that happiness is less about pursuing the external and instead focusing on the internal? A switch from inner barrenness and external pursuit to inner abundance and external containment?

While the world pauses in seducing us with the happiness of the flesh, sitting in my COVID refuge, I meander towards the inner world and what it has to offer. I marvel at the content and sequence of the wisdom Lord Krishna offered in the Gita where he spoke of the types of happiness:

> *visayendriya-samyogad yat tad agre'mrtopamam*
> *pariname visamiva tat sukham rajas am smrtam II*
>
> (*BG*, 18:38)
>
> That which appears initially like elixir through the union of senses and their objects, but in effect is like a poison, that happiness is rajasic.

- Could this be Lord Krishna awakening us to the fallacy of the pursuit of happiness where the essential premise is that happiness lies outside of us and is sought through sense gratifications?

> *yad agre chanubandhe cha sukaham mohanam atmanah*
> *nidralasya-pramadottham tat tamasam udahritam II*
>
> (*BG*, 18:39)
>
> That happiness which both initially and in the end deludes the Self, arising from sleep, laziness and inattention, that is said to be tamasic.

- Could this be Lord Krishna warning us of the falsity of the romantic idea that life is about 'eat, sleep and be merry', the driving mantra of our world in the last few years?

> *yat tad agre visamiva pariname 'mrtopamam*
> *tat sukham sattvikam proktam atma-buddhi-prasadajam II*
> (*BG,* 18:37)
>
> That which initially is like a poison but is in effect like elixir, that happiness is called sattvic, born of the pleasantness of one's intelligence.
>
> - This is Lord Krishna pointing us towards the fact that if we choose to discipline our mind and free our sight and hearing, we may awaken to the reality that true happiness is found not in the external world but within.
> - Could it also be the call towards our dharma, our duty? Could it be a call to focus on our responsibilities rather than rights and entitlements? A call for prioritizing the collective over the individual?

When the source of our delight is external, we become victims of our own attachments and aversions, which taint our happiness with sorrow. The delight soon diminishes because either the object of our happiness changes or our own notions of happiness change.

Real happiness is that which is neither disturbing nor painful. Yet, it may seem like poison for it enforces a discipline on individuals and their individuality. But in doing so it prepares them to locate the fountainhead of happiness so that they can be happy within themselves and with others.

The true meaning of happiness is the pleasantness of one's intelligence – a clear and untethered mind that finds peace and contentment. Let the museums be for the glory of our physical achievements but let happiness be the ground for our soul. Maybe it's time to step out of the pursuit of happiness, and instead, ennoble our minds to dip into the stream of inner joy, so that the pursuit of happiness can finally cease.

8

Posture

FOMO – Fear of Missing Out

We are creatures of belief. We attempt to exhibit the rectitude of our minds through our living. In doing so, over time we have come to objectify and commoditize beauty and leisure. We have named it luxury. We have come to symbolize a good life in terms of lavish holidays, luxury goods and expensive art. But the history of luxury is one of fear. We have elevated them to the status of virtues, indulged in them and then feared missing out on them.

Who can possibly correct these notions that have exalted themselves to virtues? No court of law can contest them. What could be the anti-law to incessant holidays and grandiose acquisitions in the name of a good life? What can be the tax against the sense of entitlement and the show that splurges the gains of all hard work?

There is a constant chase for something new and exciting. Not being a participant in this chase is trauma. This trauma is called FOMO, the Fear of Missing Out, and we are driven by it. Even in asking 'so what is new?', the old seems to have been deemed undesirable. But it's clear that the object of our desire is shallow and the fear of missing out on it is shallow too, as we switch to the next fashionable thing quite easily. It's true, the grass is greener on the other side – till we get to it.

But even a glass of the finest wine in hand will not conceal the hollowness of the eyes. The age of high excitement and excesses is definitely taking a toll on us, tiring us and leaving us more depleted than entertained. The ocean looks romantic till we try to swim it. Dive into the ocean and the romance quits, waiting to be placed somewhere else.

JOMO – Joy of Missing Out

With the onset of COVID, we landed up placing our belief in a grandiosity built into JOMO – the Joy of Missing Out. Was this joy or some kind of perverse consolation? Was this simply a sigh of relief? An ease that descended on people as they spoke of the endless trays of baked banana bread, tending to plants, spruced-up homes or just enjoying doing nothing? But I am not sure whether it was real joy or just relief.

It's strange how we fall short on thought and makeshift our lives. While withdrawal from excesses is a respite, disallowing ourselves the joys of everyday life is misunderstood austerity. It is not so much the object or sources of joy which are the problem but our attitude towards them. The victory is less in the transition from fear to joy, and more in taking stock of the aspect of missing out. The real joy of life is not in the extremes in any case.

Languishing

It's clear that when we humans fail to see meaning in life and get stuck in our beliefs, nature and destiny, being honest as they always are, never fail to bring home their lessons. As the world plunged into the second and more lethal wave of the pandemic, we were stripped of all our enthusiasm. Struck by horror and loss, the world has now sunk into 'languishing'.

This condition is being called the neglected middle child of mental health, where we are all feeling joyless and aimless. FOMO and JOMO are no consolation anymore. It is a sense of emptiness, a void, an indifference to indifference. A listlessness abounds.

Reflections in the Twilight Zone

The juggler must juggle very rapidly for the act to look natural. We jump hurriedly from one pleasure to the next and call it a lifestyle. The natural boredom that exists in all of us makes dedication to any one object, thought or person soon turn odious. Our attention is like a perishable commodity that seeks constant newness.

While objects and possessions have a way of exciting us till they exhaust us, experiences animate us till we return to our dullness. Yes, we do gain from our experiences – a wider horizon of knowing. But maybe 'experience' is different from experiences. A holiday with a stressed mind is more like a working day. Of what use are new experiences if the same old eyes are to see them? Borrowing from Emerson, 'Of what use to make heroic vows of amendment, if the same old law breaker is to keep them?'

Neither excitement nor suffering really gets us in touch with reality. They greet us but are soon dropped by us as our instinct for self-preservation prevails. But today we languish because we have been exhausted by both our fears and our excitements.

So, what is the way out? There seems to be a frustration in the question itself. Maybe this frustration is what will compel resolution. But no resolution will be possible until the frames of reference shift. This is not unique to our generation but has been a challenge across generations. In fact, this was the very challenge addressed by Lord Krishna when he pointed out:

> *ya nisha sarva-bhutanam tasyam jagarti sanyami*
> *yasyam jagrati bhutani sa nisha pashyato muneh*
> (*BG*, 2:69)
>
> What all beings consider as day is the night of ignorance for the wise, and what all creatures see as night is the day for the introspective sage.
>
> - At the mundane level of consciousness, material enjoyment is seen as success and deemed as the bright 'day' of life, while austerity is seen as the dark of the night. But sages have all along seen it as otherwise.
> - This verse also points to the importance of quiet and solitude. This solitude, deemed as night by the ordinary, is when the sage gathers the true blossoms of life. In solitude, the sage remains unaffected by the lure of the mundane.

The external world is alluring, but it lacks the capacity to satisfy human yearning. All events, objects, experiences and people in our lives are but a fraction of the ultimate reality, which is whole and complete. We may add up the parts and yet never know the sum; the reality or truth that we seek is the whole sum. The satisfaction we get from the parts naturally remains short of complete. FOMO and JOMO remain notional.

In not knowing our true reality, we search for reality outside us. We wish to anchor to it but eventually realize that the anchorage is nothing but quicksand. When neither extreme satisfies, we languish in the twilight zone. As its greatest gift, languishing is a zone of opportunities – provided we comprehend it as such.

Life as a Posture

There is a good way of doing everything even if it is just slicing bread. Whatever be the way, the good will emerge only from a stillness that will hold it. The privilege of touching reality belongs to those who strive for it. And the striving required is unlikely to come from will, but rather, from the invitations of stillness.

Needing is the law for all who are not in self-possession. Our struggle continues because we all fall into the trap of forgetfulness. Forgetting that we are everything, we fear being nothing. Alas, in vain, we keep the futile struggle to be at least something.

All neediness ceases when we are in possession of our higher Self – which reveals itself in stillness. There is no better source of this wisdom than the *Yoga Sutra*:

> *sthirasukham asanam*
> (*YS*, 2:46)
>
> A stable and comfortable posture is asana.
>
> - This short and terse verse holds all the wisdom to remedy the aftermath of any global or personal crisis. In situations of overexcitement or fear, stability is lost. And comfort is lost when we are constantly provoked or agitated.
> - In yogic literature, *asana* means posture, and any posture is inherently about balancing the inner forces.
> - We are a composite of our body and mind, and nothing is nearer to us. All our wealth is buried in our body and mind.
> - The irony is that even though we are born with an infinite wealth of vigour, vitality, beauty and power, we search for it outside. According to yogic wisdom, re-establishing this inner connection begins with asana.
> - An asana is mastered when we achieve stability and comfort in it.

Stillness is not passive. It is dynamic and tidal. It is palpable and can be seen in the way we hold ourselves. It is the posture we hold as we inhabit this world and interact with it. Touching reality is the prerogative of a still mind.

JOMI – Joy of Moving In

The whole economy of nature is built on the way it expresses itself. It sways in happiness, anchored to its own being. The cure to languishing will come from first finding our stillness – the quality such that when I am measured at first glance, I measure up to my highest possibility.

I believe that all the offers of pleasure and displeasure will be forgotten once the senses holiday in the peace of the soul. JOMI, or the Joy of Moving In – moving inwards into stillness, is the posture which will be the perfect antidote to all the FOMO, JOMO and languishing.

9

Hidden Revelation

Which is that one question which can never really be asked of another?

Consider the question: 'Who am I?' Imagine the absurdity of my placing this question in front of another and asking them to tell me who I am! Seeking an answer to this question is evidently a solo exercise. And perhaps the question itself begins to invite the answer, as I was soon to find out.

One day as I was negotiating some unruly drivers on the road, I got myself stuck in a rather stubborn, nerve-wrenching traffic jam, typical of Delhi. While the lyrics of Leonard Cohen soothed my ears, I found myself looking into the rear-view mirror and staring at my own face. At first glance, my face looked familiar, but as I continued to look and read newer details, it began to change. I kept looking, only to find that my own eyes were looking back at me, and soon I was watching my eyes watching me. Then, in the lingering moments, my attention shifted to how I was thinking about my own looks. And eventually, as I persisted, my eyes and mind grew a bit tired and all I experienced was me sitting behind the wheel looking into the mirror.

As the traffic gave way, I began to drive in low gear, recognizing this moment of epiphany; the answer to 'who am I' can rarely be found in language and words, instead, it clearly lies in experience. It was like when you read a map well and begin to get a sense of the territory. I was reading my face and getting a sense of who I am.

As I drove on, I began to feel a lightness. It was the lightness that comes when after negotiating a rough journey, the destination appears in front of you – the moment when Google Maps says, 'You have arrived at your destination' and you bring the car to a halt with a sigh of relief.

In that lightness, the question I had carried for a while was now meeting its answer. It became clear that the answer to 'Who am I?' comes through an experience in which 'presence' is felt. This presence is who I am.

In that moment, amidst the high traffic, I had a glimpse of myself seated in my own presence. As my introspection deepened, this presence, which is the foundational wisdom of the Vedic scriptures I have been a student of, began to slowly and systematically unravel.

Self-Knowledge

It dawned on me that Self-knowledge is a highly elusive phenomenon and can never really be the final answer to the question I was asking. It is merely a series of 'shifting frames'.

Firstly, when I begin to see and know myself, what I know is just a fragment of my totality. I know what I see. But I am yet to know all that I still can't see. While my physicality is visible, my thoughts and emotions are less readable. So much lies in the unseen, unspoken, the hidden and the unexplored.

Secondly, the problem seems to amplify because although I may expand my knowledge, what I know ceases to be so the moment after I have known it. Let's say I look within to know myself. As I do so, I see and recognize a trait about myself. Now, am I the same? Or, am I what I was minus one layer of ignorance? To that extent, by simply seeing myself, I have changed. What I know of myself is not what I am in the present moment. How elusive this makes the notion of Self-knowledge! Many a time I have sat on the banks of the Ganga in Varanasi and watched the river. But do I know it? Probably not. What I do know is how the Ganga looks in flow – ever-changing perhaps.

Self-knowledge is acknowledging that as I understand, I change, and so I never permanently know! Everything I know, I know in the moment; but the moment itself being transient, vanishes into the past as soon as I acknowledge it.

Finally, if 'I' can understand the 'Self' then I need to be bigger than the Self, because I can only understand what is within my grasp. And grasping something implies that it is smaller than the grasper. This leaves us with an open-ended question – is there any one of us that understands the Self?

Self-Inquiry

Acknowledging that Self-knowledge does not allow for the dynamism of real life, I open myself up to further curiosity and exploration – a dive within. Could the journey of knowing the Self be a process of Self-inquiry?

The first frontier is understanding that a dive within rests on the recognition of inward and outward. While the world is external, the mind is internal, so the body serves as a threshold.

So far, all I know is the physicality of my body and what I see through the lens of my mind. So, Self-inquiry is first and foremost, inquiring into the structure and workings of this body–mind apparatus. Let me borrow from Shankaracharya's *Drig Drishya Viveka* to bring clarity to this debate:

> *rupam drishyam locanam drik tad drishyam drik tu manasam*
> *drishya dhi-vrittayah sakshi drig eva na tu drishyate II*
> (*DDV*, V:1)
>
> The form is perceived and the eye is its perceiver
> It (eye) is perceived and the mind is its perceiver
> The mind with its modifications is perceived and the witness (Self) is verily the perceiver
> But it (the Self) is not perceived by any other.

Mostly we recognize only what we can see. As a child, for me, the stars were closer than my grandmother's house in the neighbouring town, simply because I could see the stars and not her house. But a concerted inquiry would entail recognition of the fact that there is a lot that exists beyond what I can see. It is placing attention where it wasn't. It is participating and coming to know the ways in which I think and feel. It is knowing how I exist. For how many moments am I happy or unhappy and how much support does my happiness need?

While I may decide to see with a wider gaze, the seeing becomes an effort because my eyes and senses get distracted and tired, while my mind gets conditioned and turns into an unclean mirror, which verily reflects distorted images.

But equally, there is acknowledgement of what lies in the dark. As I begin to see and observe what Carl Jung called the shadow, I begin to recognize that a shadow can exist only as long as there is a form, a reality to support it. Self-inquiry is knowing that as I change my shape and edges, the shape of my shadow will also change. It is to understand that we live on the threshold of light and dark. It is to recognize that till I am embodied, I will cast a shadow, however small and varying it maybe. In a way, it is a conformation of my incarnation.

Self-Forgetting

But are my incarnation and its shadow really me? They may both be mine but are they me? What may be needed is to put aside what I am not. Possibly some amount of Self-forgetting is warranted? In doing so, maybe what is there will eventually reveal itself.

I begin to recognize that there must be something propelling the mind and the body. I call that the 'Self'. But the key question is: How do I go into 'my Self' to know it? It's the classic problem of the eyes not being able to see themselves or the tongue not being able to taste itself. How does the 'Self' know itself?

The solution probably lies in looking at all that I am not, and putting all that aside. Ramana Maharshi's famous *'neti-neti'*, that is, 'not this-not this' is brought into focus. I am not the body nor its possessions; I am not the thoughts and emotions; I am not the mind. Then who am I?

As I chip away at all that is not me, I merge into a kind of nothingness – a kind of Self-forgetting. An onion with its layers peeled seems non-existent. But this Self-forgetting is what allows an inner essence to reveal itself – like a sculptor who chips away at a block of stone till the statue reveals itself. And so, chipped of all that it is not, the true Self reveals itself.

Self-Knowing

The true Self reveals itself as an experience – a Self-knowing. It is knowing not by doing or perceiving, but by being. The real foundation of the Self is not Self-knowledge; it is the knowing that emerges from Self-knowledge, Self-inquiry and Self-forgetting. Self-knowing is knowing the nature of my existence as an experience – not as an object, nor as perception and not even an absence. It is a presence. Eloquently explained in the *Drig Drishya Viveka* as:

> *nodeti nastametyesa na vrddhim yati na ksayam*
> *svayam vibhatyathanyani bhasayetsadhanam vina II*
> (*DDV*, V:5)
>
> This 'I' (witness) does not arise nor does it set. It does not increase nor decrease. It shines by itself and its light illumines others without any external aid.
>
> - To know the ever-changing world, there must be an unchanging reality. It seems obvious that anything that is unchanging will be outside the scope of time and space – the reference points we use to help us understand anything. So herein lies the problem of understanding the Self. It is beyond reference points.
> - The verse also says that this reality shines of itself. What will shine of itself will naturally be Self-knowing. And it will be the very principle by which all will be known.

As inner luminosity illumines my reality, it also allows me to know the nature of life and my place in it. I know life only as it happens through me. I begin by knowing my body–mind apparatus as that is what is most real to me. But then, this itself becomes the doorway to a higher knowing.

Self-knowing is also understanding that while the form casts a shadow, the same in its pristine state, may radiate a halo. But how would I, an ordinary mortal being radiate a halo?

The *Yoga Sutra* clarifies this in as much as it emphasizes it to be the acid test for Self-knowing:

> *svadhyayadistadevatasamprayogah II*
> (*YS*, 2:44)
>
> From Self-study comes the opportunity to be in the company of bright beings (of our choice).

- The *Yoga Sutra* clearly spells out that through Self-study and Self-knowing which is a fruit thereof, we begin to radiate the halo – the essential brilliance of the bright or higher beings we choose to imbibe.
- This is because as our mirror gets totally cleaned up, we comprehend and connect with our higher selves in direct proportion to the quality and capacity of our pure mind.

Through this process we are in the full view of our higher Self as it is in ours. Just as we know that the sun is shining even on a cloudy day, we continue to experience the subtle counterparts of our own divine radiance. And this is what we, in turn, radiate outward – the transformational power of inner luminosity. Self-knowing is the halo I exude.

All said and done, as I sit in self-reflection, I come to get a sense of the fact that Self-knowing is the Self-luminosity in which all is known. The sense of presence I felt sitting in my car the other day, watching my face in the mirror, was nothing but my own inherent Self-luminosity.

Words seem inadequate to describe the full expanse of the Self which lies in an experience. Experiencing this presence has been the rightful destination of my journey. In a way every experience points me back to myself. I stand hidden, yet revealed in experience.

10

The Solitude of Strength

Today I spent the day cleaning up my make-up drawer. It was the moment to pay tribute to a scatter of lipsticks which saw their demise gradually over the last 18 months of COVID. Singing a requiem to them as I placed them in the trash can, I wondered what new hues would surface post-COVID. Colours have a way of representing moods and I wondered which colours would come to represent the muted and nude reality of these times.

Over the years, one of my greatest joys has been to go shopping with friends, and buying a lipstick was integral to the list. But this was seeming like a somewhat distant reality – a waiting. Life was definitely becoming solitary and meeting friends an infrequent treat. In that solitude, my books began beckoning to me. Frequently, a book languishing on my bookshelf for years would catch my attention, wanting to be picked up and befriended. Heeding one such call, I retrieved a book in high black gloss with echoes from the past – *Audrey Hepburn (Icons of Our Time Series)* –

Referred to as hard-working, adorable, delightful and natural, what she came to represent was 'style'. Looking over her pictures, what sprang to attention, beyond her lipstick and the simplicity of her iconic dress sense, was the strength of her innocence and her rhythmic grace. Ticking off a complaining cameraman one day, she had asserted, 'I am just me. I am what I am, and I haven't done too badly like this.' This, to my mind, is what made her a style icon and not a fashion brand. All this was causing a question to form in my mind: Can I claim to know my style?

Amidst the mayhem of COVID and a new stage of life which was anyway an invitation to realign myself to life, I became acutely aware of a silence, which I was beginning to live with. The solitude of these times was an offer to construct a new vocabulary for the Self – to cultivate my style afresh. What was the ordering of time calling out for? What would my proclamation of 'I am what I am' stand on?

There is a depth to living that needs to be known and mastered. In recognizing this, I began to choose and construct my own constituency – my solitude of strength.

Honesty

Being truthful had been about accepting fear, helplessness and vulnerability. It was less about speaking the truth and more about acknowledging how jagged its lines had become and how fearful I had been of facing it.

Nature hides neither disease nor decay and there was no rationale for me to hide the dark and darkened in me either. The effort to hide or deny our inner truths and instead put up a grandiose front can be wearying, and often strips us of inner congruity. Honesty is a situation where thoughts, speech and actions are well integrated and not at variance with each other. Honesty is congruence, an inner alignment.

The weight of truth is not measured in grams or kilograms but in the fact that it eventually beckons the heart to its side and finds a way of speaking through us. Honesty and inner congruity allow for the mind to become serene and words to be spoken with kindness. When I am one with myself, I am at peace with myself and the world.

Courage

It takes courage to be honest. For me, it was the declaration to reset and embark on a more courageous road. It was a commitment to isolation, anxiety, fluidity and unknowing – a mustering of courage for the annihilation of a known identity. The dead weight of old identities has little bearing on the emergent reality. The personhood must cease for the person to emerge.

Courage, coming from its root word 'cor', is about learning to speak from the heart. It was thus a decision to live with an open heart; no matter how much it would bleed or tremble, I prayed that this decision which began with fluidity would end up creating the most solid and stable ground – a ground of inner knowing.

This process warranted vigilance. When looking into the mirror, there are moments when you want to escape yourself. But in staying, it is precisely this desire that becomes the doorway to expansion. It was overcoming the fearful avoidance of the unknown and the uncomfortable, which I felt I was not equal to. And in this very overcoming lay the equalization.

The natural world demonstrates this equalization in many ways but the one that is most striking is the transformation of the caterpillar into the butterfly. The caterpillar will die if it does not transform; its evolution lies in its transformation. And, in turn, its transformation lies in dissolution. Turning itself into the chrysalis, the self-woven cocoon in which it dissolves, it again transforms itself to rise as a butterfly. In its dissolution, it touches its essence. This essence remains the common thread between the caterpillar and the butterfly.

Two facts warrant attention here. First, what seems like dissolution and possible loss is, in fact, the material from which the metamorphosis is enabled. The death of the caterpillar is itself the raw material for the birth of the butterfly. So, the butterfly does not bemoan the loss of its old Self; instead, it celebrates its renewal. Second, post-dissolution, what gets carried forward is the essence itself. Essence is what always remains.

Unlike the caterpillar where nature assists and leads the way, I knew that as a conscious being, I had the courage and capacity to mindfully walk the path of my own transformation.

Acceptance

Acceptance of how life was unfolding was necessary for me to move forward. It was the point at which my struggle ceased to be. A state where we are brought down to our knees, but the gift of the moment is that we begin to feel the ground underneath – a firmer sense of Self. Acceptance is the space in which fears transmute into will and determination. A space from which emerges generosity in the assessment of oneself and others.

The Solitude of Strength

What is there to not accept? Once we accept the fact that what is happening was meant to happen, that it is the way in which individual and collective *karma* is to play out, then that acceptance is the beginning of a pilgrimage. A journey to an answer that lies beyond the known Self. It is acknowledging the heartbreak and the helpless in life. It is making the decision to walk on, in sweet pain, with realigned steps.

When the journey is honest and blessed, the right guidance does appear. Here's a verse from the Bhagavad Gita that sprang to attention:

> *amanitvam adambhitvam ahinsa kshantir arjavam*
> *acharyopasanam shaucham sthairyam atma-vinigrahah II*
> (*BG*, 13:8)
>
> Humility, honesty, non-violence, patience, simplicity, service to the teacher, purity, stillness and restraint are declared to be knowledge in practice.
>
> - These qualities are about putting our knowledge of how to live into practice.
> - These are virtues of a wise aspirant.

The above verse became my guiding light, the yardstick based on which I decided to take my journey forward. It was guiding me to put away all attributes of pride, anger, judgement and restlessness, and instead adopt courage, honesty, wisdom, faith, purity and resolve. These were going to be the beads of my garland. I knew that anything that was unspoken or unresolved would resolve in this knowing.

What becomes most important is to hold the right conversation of life. This requires a brave participation. Shaping the conversation was shaping the way I was taking on the act of living my life. This was to become my solitude of strength, the firm ground from where I was going to have a greater abidance in 'I am who I am'.

11

Bead by Bead

Acquiring patience has been a very personal journey for me. Somewhere between confidence, yearning, anxiety and the judgement of youth, and the temperance of life and age, the doorway to patience stood waiting to be opened.

In the last few years, COVID has certainly tested our patience. It has brought all of us to a point where we have no option but to live each day as it comes with all its mundane details. I have delighted in cooking new dishes, finding new ways to cook them and even spent time appreciating the freshness of my morning papaya and bananas. But gradually I began to realize that engaging with the mundane has something extraordinary about it. It is the point when the rested in us beckons the restless in us. The preferred language of this interaction is patience.

Isn't patience the only ground on which a steady and sane future can be built? If one looks around, it is not hard to spot. The making of human character and strength happens over time – built over nights of dark and quiet striving. It is the law that I see hold in all the people I admire.

Patience helps us touch that which is beyond us. Three years of patience and hard work led Edison to the lightbulb. And according to the French cosmologist, naturalist, and mathematician C. Buffon, 'Genius is only a greater aptitude for patience.'

Also, 'If I have made any valuable discoveries, it has been owing more to patient attention than any other talent,' said Isaac Newton.

Life requires time, and nothing robs life more than haste. I notice the patience with which the earth swelters through the scorching Indian summer, waiting for the dryness to be moistened by the first rain. Its relief is palpable, fragranced with newness.

I revel in those friendships which have stood the test of time, and know that no friendship can be cultivated without the long, waving hand of time.

Patience with Oneself

Living this moment of unknowing and searching is patience. It is when I let the worms of my thoughts and feelings come to the contemplation of my inner knowing. It is being patient with the questioned and the unanswered. It is waiting for a clarity to evolve, knowing the waiting is difficult to measure in time. After all, the flowering of a bud is not denominated in time.

Patience is the ground on which the restlessness of the moment resides and resolves. The gift of patience is our ability to straddle time. It is an opportunity to gather, be it peace, understanding, an inner clarity, or freedom – the beads that string themselves and become our garland of virtues. But then it stays in me as the blood of my ancestors does at every meandering of my life.

There is a softness to patience; it becomes a comfort on the pathway to the future. Bit by bit, it leads us to integrate the new that approaches us, until nothing alien and uncomfortable remains. It allows for the silent embrace of fate, and provides solace as we come to inhabit that fate with serenity.

Lord Krishna, pointing towards the same, says:

> *shamo damas tapah ahaucham kshantir arjavam eva cha*
> *jnanam vijnanam astikyam brahma-karma svabhava-jam*
> (*BG*, 18:42)
>
> Tranquility, restraint, austerity, purity, patience, integrity, knowledge, wisdom and faith are the intrinsic qualities of work for a Brahmin.
>
> - It is a false notion that a person is a Brahmin (learned) merely by birth. A true quest and Self-effort renders one a Brahmin.
> - Integral to the purer qualities is the quality of *kshanti* (patience). It is the quality that anchors all other qualities.
> - Kshanti is the will to wait.

While kshanti is patience, the other quality embedded in it is forgiveness. Patience is the forbearance of Stephen Hawkins as also the forgiveness of Christ. It is accepting the present and releasing the past such that the future is secured. It is the story of Isaac Newton and his dog Diamond who destroyed thirty years of his effort in a moment. All Newton did was sigh, and get down to rewriting his work.

Patience becomes a cultivated way of life. A way that allows us to master both our internal and external worlds. As we expand, in our expansion, our understanding of and ability to interact with the world also grows.

Patience with the World

The thread of patience has to be woven gently. It is a state of equilibrium – uninfluenced by passion or ignorance – from where we can relate constructively to the outer world.

A lack of patience creates plenty of collateral damage. Consider Alexander and his Gordian Knot – when unable to untie the knot, he sliced it off and set it free. While this was a display of power, unfortunately what was also lost in the bargain was the connection and connectivity. The rope, having been cut into many parts in one go, stood shortened, and was never the same again. In much the same way, the lack of patience severs the connection between us and others, and cannibalizes much of what has been built over time. Patience has a certain softness that allows for connection and continuity to be retained.

The most difficult people in our lives are our greatest teachers. Patience means leaning into their teaching rather than focusing on their words. It is a reminder that we are being challenged to look further and strengthen ourselves, without letting our hearts get hardened.

Instead of retaliation, patience means refraining from setting up targets for others to attack us. It is keeping our seat and not reacting. It is not adding heat to an already burning fire, and instead dousing it with the coolness of the heart while maintaining purpose. It is the practised life of Mahatma Gandhi, the Dalai Lama and Nelson Mandela.

Growing into Patience

Maybe, later is actually better so that we are ready for it? Patience is waiting; critical in our world of instant gratification where value gets lost in the haste. I wonder, why wait if we have to do so miserably, complainingly, nervously or in frustration? Yet the wisdom is to know, as in the words of Rilke, 'Everything must be carried to term before it is born.' Seems we have the promise, and all we have to do is grow into it.

Patience is a quiet waiting in faith. As I write these words, I reflect on the words of my spiritual teacher, who has been gently advising me to be patient and allow life to flow within the sweeping hands of time. Equally, he has encouraged me, in the meanwhile, to commit myself to regular practice and reflection, always emphasizing that it is only over the thread of patience that we can string the beads of our character. Today, I realize that patience is not just a word, it's a path. Patience is not passive – it is an active surrender. There is no despair in patience. We wait courageously and knowingly – trusting what is good, will come.

We have to determine to be patient. Unfortunately, when we don't and instead act out of impatience and aggression, our inner voice of knowing begins to soften and then quieten. It is not in its nature to be loud. It drowns in the noise of our mental cacophony and the din of external opinions and judgements. The determination to be patient challenges our endurance. To open the knots, we must tread with patience.

A person with character will have many characteristics, but the very strength of the character lies in something that traverses silently and significantly throughout the person – a deep patience.

Patience lends itself to binding the character. It is the doorway that grants permission to proceed, without ever bringing itself to attention. It is like the iron string that lays itself out as a long and unbroken thread on which beads of the garland are strung – bead by bead.

12

Respectful

It was a relaxed Sunday morning and I had the songs from my R&B and Soul playlist filtering through the house. Settling into my couch, I reached for the newspaper and soon the headlines had me rapt. The killing of people of colour and the 'Me–Too' movement had taken centre stage. As I was devouring the headlines, I was brought to a pause when the song 'Respect' by Aretha Franklin began to play.

'Respect' had been recorded in 1967 and it became an anthem of sorts – a demand for something that could no longer be denied. The popularity of the song lay in its ingenuity and boldness. It was a call for equality and mutual respect. The artiste took a man's demand for respect from his woman when he came home from work and simply turned it over. The lyrics were now about a woman demanding respect when the man came home. It shook and jolted the conditioned thinking of that era.

But whosever perspective one sees it from, it is clear that across times and generations, respect has been an important theme. An inherent human need exhibiting itself; a cry of the minority and a demand by the majority.

Respect as a Demand

What we have seen through the annals of history is the wielding of power and demand for respect in the name of monarchy, patriarchy, seniority, and even knowledge. What really drives this demand? This demand for power which in itself is based on inequality, has the more powerful person demanding it, and the weaker person yearning for it. An entitlement of sorts. In fact, could the constant demand for respect be a cry for control and a need to establish authority? Could it be a call of desperation, the loss of self-autonomy? Respect lies in the realm of the psychological world rather than the material world. Hitler, Stalin and many other leaders – the monsters of history – have all been victims of this hunger, a kind of neurosis.

Can respect be linked to value? If I were to look at my relationship with money, I would find that while I value money, I find it difficult to say that I respect it. Maybe because money at best is the means to an end, and not the end in itself. But the value proposition rests on the notion of satisfaction. And satisfaction is derived when the end is met. The end is the satisfaction of need and thereby the cessation of that need. So, can there be a possible equation between need and respect? Do we respect things we need, or is respect a need in itself?

Immanuel Kant was right to put the focus of respect on the person because he treated the person as the end. This took the debate around respect into the realm of morals. But on deeper reflection, a person is nothing but a composite of 'needs'. Could it be the need to feel important and valued, which is transacted at the level of respect? And maybe acceptance, appreciation, caring, attention, kindness and gratitude are the currency of this transaction. Was this the cry in Aretha Franklin's words?

Respect Earned

A currency is notional unless backed, a need is unmet unless satisfied, and respect is nominal unless earned. To 'earn' as per its epistemology, means to merit, labour for, to harvest or to reap. Earning respect would mean labouring for it and harvesting it.

Lord Krishna in the Gita prompts Arjuna to do his duty by going into battle and thereby earning his honour and respect:

> *akirtim chapi bhutani kathayishyanti te 'vyayam*
> *sambhavitasya chakirtir maranad atirichyate II*
> (*BG* 2:34)
>
> People will speak inglorious things about you and such ill repute for someone once honoured is worse than death.
>
> - When a person ignores his duties, others think disparagingly of him.

Lord Krishna reminds Arjuna that as a warrior, it is his duty to fight, or he will lose his honour. Since our duty is defined by social constructs, respect is earned in its discharge within the same context.

It may be useful to ponder the fact that if we conduct ourselves according to our life stage and its personal or professional duties, it may be the way to labour for and harvest respect.

Taking this argument further, the call of duty and its discharge may seem simplistic on the surface, but it involves skills, attitudes, conduct, wisdom and dispositions, all braided together. The ability to garner and braid them would need a lifetime's labour, and sum up to harvesting a lifetime's earnings. The beauty of respect is that we don't wait till the end of life to harvest it, but do so every day of our lives. How dynamic this process is! Does it not merit its earning?

Respect for the Self

Self-respect is essentially the relationship a person has with themselves, which is based on the need for self-worth. This, in turn, may accrue from membership and status, as well as agency and autonomy. But whatever be the source, it is vital to the experienced quality of our lives and is worth striving for.

But do we really know what we are talking about when we talk of self-respect? Respect is a transaction and any transaction can only be between 'two'. Could the New Age obsession with self-respect be the dangerous condition where a person has disintegrated into two within himself, and now there is a transaction between his two halves? This tussle between the true-Self and ego-Self might have the makings of a neurosis. A situation where the need for integration of the Self is misrepresented as an unforgiving and uncompromising demand for respect from another person? And in the event of not getting it, translates into anger and resentment?

For the composite creature called a human being, self-respect may in essence be about an inner congruence that reverberates and enlivens the Self.

> Number one in your life's blueprint should be a deep belief in your own dignity, your own worth, and your own somebody-ness ... if you can't be the sun, be a star, be the best at whatever you are.
>
> (Martin Luther King Jr.)

Respectful

This inner congruence, being the best versions of ourselves, may be the sacred space where no transactions are warranted. It is the congruity of our thought–speech–action through which we honour ourselves and, which in turn, commands its own respect.

Respectfulness

The same sacred space may exist even in relation to others, where respect may actually have no transactional dimension. It may be purely an inner quality, a state of looking towards the other.

Can I call it a virtue? Virtue is less about moral excellence and more about knowing who we really are. But being virtuous is quite different from becoming virtuous. Cultivated virtues may bring respectability but won't beget respect.

So maybe respect can be seen as a living practice rather than a transaction. A practice that one lives every day and in doing so, inhabits the space it creates. As we live it every day, by doing so we become our practice itself. What the pathway to such a practice could be is clearly delineated in the *Yoga Sutra*:

> *sa tu dirghakalanairantaryasatkarasevito drdha-bhumih II*
>
> (*YS*, 1:14)
>
> It becomes firm when done for a long period of time, with no interruption and with reverence.

The gem hidden in this sutra is one of *satkara* (reverence). The sense of reverence is a hard-earned one. The elements of satkara as enlisted by this wisdom are given below.

Tapas

Essentially, the ability to conquer resistance to practice itself. Seen in our context, the ability to be polite, reverential, conforming, law-abiding, are all austerities on the path of respect.

Brahmacharya

Usually misunderstood as celibacy, but the heart of it is Self-discipline that leads to mastery over the senses and thus empowers internal congruence. It would, through a subtle effect, promote looking towards the higher dimensions of life. This would allow for virtues to grow unimpeded.

Vidya

It is the understanding where one knows the nature of the world and its objects, and knows our relationships to them. Accepting the polarities and differences, acknowledging our interdependence, we come to possibly understand the 'is-ness' of life. Equally, it is the process of knowing our relationship with ourselves and our own fullness.

Shraddha

The joyous state of mind that stems from abiding faith where all fears and doubts dissipate.

Satkara

This is the womb in which all of life is revered and nourished; the womb itself is prepared through a lifetime of effort.

Why are children taught to respect their parents? It's not so much because the parents deserve respect, but because by inducting oneself into the practice of respect continuously over a long period of time, what is cultivated is a sense of respect. This sense when combined with satkara, evolves into deep respectfulness.

As the words of the song echoed in my ear, what rang loud is that the essence of respect lies in respectfulness. Respectfulness is a state of being. A state where we look at the world around us with acceptance, gratitude and appreciation. A beingness where possibly everything is a privilege and all demands and transactions cease to be.

Clean and Dirty

Sitting with my cup of coffee and savouring a slice of cake, I am shaken out of my comfort. I read news of funeral pyres in Delhi as the city puts up a brave but unsuccessful fight for oxygen amidst the ravages of COVID. The pleasure I get from my coffee and my anguish at witnessing human suffering stand face to face. I struggle to watch them with an equal gaze. In that moment, I recognize the pleasure of my pleasure as well as the anguish of my anguish; yet, I stand in a space of discomfort. It is from this discomfort that I am attempting to see both.

Everyone seems temperamental these days, including the weather. It had been hot for a few days and it seemed the Indian summer was ready to unleash its scorch. The trees looked dry and dusty as if they needed a good wash. To cheer us in our captivity, the rain gods relented and it has been pouring for the last 24 hours. I sit on my patio relishing the newly bathed look of the trees, but as I look down and see my patio floor, I see a scatter of fallen leaves and dirt and water waiting to find their way into the drains. I see the heavens looking clean but the earth seeming dirty, in the same moment.

Clean and Dirty

Enjoying the weather, I invite my mother to join me for coffee and a piece of toast. As we engage in an interesting conversation, I notice that age makes us creatures of habit. When I offer her a bite, she expresses her desire to have the left edge of the toast as always. I notice that what remains along the line of divide after giving her the left edge, is still the left.

Taking away the left side does not give me the right side, as there can be no right without its corresponding left. The left and right can never be separated as one exists only in reference to the other. I can see one side not in the absence of the other, but in parallel with it. I wonder why; if so much of our life draws attention to the parallels in it, do we struggle to see and understand things only in their separateness? Could it be that as you read this script, it is possible to decipher the black alphabets only against the light background?

Is it possible for us to see the background and foreground simultaneously as parallel?

While it is possible, it is not the design of our seeing. This is because our attention has difficulty in seeing both sides at once. If you stand to my 'right' and say something to me, I am likely to turn my head towards you along with my attention. In that moment, the parallel 'left' is bereft of my attention and lapses into otherness. It is the same play that happens between the background and foreground too.

Can I really understand a wave if I don't see its peaks and troughs as parallel? Have you ever closely looked at the yin-yang symbol? While it looks like it has a divide of black and white, the difference stands out because, along the middle S curve, the black is outlined with white and the white is outlined with black – one arising from the other. A perceptual illusion lending a palpable sense of separateness.

Possibly, there is no line that divides laughter and pain either. Doesn't a lot of human anguish stem from this unseeing? The problem seems to be that what we see, we deem as 'something' and what we don't see, we deem as 'nothing'. And then we are caught in the judgement of the something being good and the nothing being bad. All our likes and aversions stem from this. What we like gives us joy and what we dislike gives us pain. But it is for us to realize that there is no winner in this game because the sensation of more can only be against the sensation of less. For sensation is simply awareness of contrast. Life is not an either-or game. It's like when playing peekaboo, we don't hide 'or' seek, we hide 'and' seek.

This is what Lord Krishna in the Bhagavad Gita points towards whilst encouraging Arjuna to rise beyond the notions of pain and pleasure and fight the battle:

> *matra-sparsha tu kaunteya shitoshna-sukha-dukha-dah*
> *agamapayina nityas tans-titikshasva bharata II*
>
> (*BG*, 2:14)
>
> The contact between the elements, O Son of Kunti,
> are the causes of heat, cold, pleasure and pain.
> Being non-eternal, these come and go; learn to
> withstand them, O Descendant of Bharata.

Clean and Dirty

> - The contact between the senses and sense objects gives rise to fleeting perceptions of happiness and distress. These resultant emotions are non-permanent and come and go like the winter and summer. One must learn to see them with an equal gaze.

In seeing them with an equal gaze, should I tolerate them both, or is there a better way of viewing them? I seem to have landed on the knowing while doing my breath work. Sitting up on my yoga mat, as I begin to consciously breathe, I begin to recognize the presence of my inhalation and exhalation. While I recognize them as different, soon they coalesce into one single entity and I find myself held in that oneness – a flow. I don't simply tolerate the difference; instead, while accepting and appreciating them both, I begin to enjoy what lies beyond the difference.

Once again, Lord Krishna indicates that through wisdom we gain the ability to see all as non-different. We see them with an equal gaze – *samatvam* (equanimity):

> *vidya-vinaya-sampanne brahmane gavi hastini*
> *Shuni chaiva shva-pake cha panditah sama-darshina II*
> (*BG*, 5:18)
>
> The truly learned see with equal vision a Brahmin, a cow, an elephant, a dog and a dog-eater.

In the way all waves, in essence, are water, in all of the above lifeforms what we see is life – the essence, which is the same for all. Seeing and appreciating the essence begets humility. It ceases to be mere tolerance and evolves into acceptance.

As I continue to sip my coffee, I pen the thoughts running through my mind:

> How many flowers have you spotted,
> Are they all equally dotted?
> How many trees have you seen bent,
> Is it the same direction to which they have their ear lent?
> How many mountains have you seen stand,
> Are they draped the same whilst looking so grand?
> How many stones have you seen,
> Do they all have the same sheen?
> How many waves have you counted,
> Did they have the same ripples as they mounted?
> How many pens have you seen roll,
> Do they always create the same scroll?
>
> Should we create similarity in all,
> Or celebrate the differences above all??

Like a wise person once told me, even the garbage bin in its right place is divine. So maybe it's not about the 'clean or dirty' but rather about 'clean *and* dirty'. This takes away the treacherous burden of choice and lands us in the relief camp of equanimity and beyond that, appreciation.

14

Beyond Boundaries

It seems that the concept of work–life balance has shifted frames in the last two years. With COVID and the relentless lockdowns, it has been less about work from home and more about work and home. It has become the sudden inclusion of my dog's bark or my child's face on the screen as I participated in an important work meeting on Zoom. The boundaries of work and home have blurred and renegotiation is in order.

In much the same way, if we are to look at the animal kingdom, its denizens live in a happy existence where few definitions are needed, let alone boundaries. They know nothing about opposites, nor about choice or decision-making. They follow instincts alone. I am not sure if my dog goes around segregating home and work, or classifying other dogs as ugly or beautiful. Nor do rivers deem themselves virtuous or non-virtuous. Apology has no place in that world as there are no rights and wrongs there. What is there in the natural kingdom are big variations of size and colour, but these bear no judgement.

But what fate has our world of definitions and boundaries borne?

Boundaries

Ours is a measured world. We name, number and group in an attempt to segregate, in order to comprehend the equation of our world. We hit upon the unknowns and call them variables. To make meaning more refined, we define, categorize and conclude. Each step yields us more knowledge and control, yet the more we carve out segregations and boundaries, the more the knife seems to cut out the equation itself. What we fail to consider when seeing the two ends of a stick is that they are deeply connected by the stick itself.

It's true that the map is not the territory. The earth has no natural boundaries. We draw lines and boundaries to map and measure the earth. Divisions are not marked by the line; instead, it is the line that divides and manufactures the segregation. Nations and national boundaries have been the artwork of these lines. The line wields its power through the fact that it divides.

The world of division naturally lends itself to becoming a world of conflict. The line that divides also unwittingly becomes the firing line. Individual interests, be they of nations, regions, corporates, or even individuals, all stem from a division that invites otherness. The deeper the groove our knife cuts, the deeper the divide and more the anguish.

But where does the real error lie? It seems the error of judgement lies in treating the line as real and then resting our loyalty on one side of the otherness. Sorrow ensues when we attempt to manoeuvre one of the two sides. In trying to eliminate the negative, we lose the possibility of enjoying the positive. In zipping my suitcase such that nothing falls out, nothing new can be accommodated either.

Our self-identity, our ego, is the boundary line we draw upon ourselves. Where we draw the line defines the expanse of our identity. The closer it is drawn to the body–mind apparatus, the narrower our identity, and the more the soul gets segregated. Most battles are battles of the soul.

Should these lines remain lines of division or can they become lines of unification? Maybe this was the powerful image that Robert Frost evoked in one of his poems:

> ... Before I built a wall I'd ask to know
> What I was walling in or walling out,
> And to whom I was like to give offence.
> (Robert Frost, *Mending Walls*)

Unity

Is it possible to have lines of distinction but not of separation or division?

Hidden behind the explicit lies the entire world of the implicit. A world full of possibilities and connectedness. The economic model of a 'market' rests on the meeting of the demand and supply curves. They may be distinct, but they are not inseparable. In fact, the point of intersection is what permits the market to exist in the first place. While they distinguish, they form the unified whole.

In our personal context, growth fundamentally entails the relinquishing of the ego and the expansion of one's boundaries. This expansion allows for and respects the interdependence of all. The concave exists within the convex; the valley is not without the mountains.

In wanting to mark and define ourselves, we cultivate our sense of agency. But our sense of agency diminishes the value of support from others and our mutual interdependence. Maybe the very power of agency is a support given to us by something beyond us and much larger than us? What could that something larger be?

Lord Krishna directs us to this ultimate unity and support:

> *ishvarah sarva-bhutanam hrid-deshe 'rjuna tishthati*
> *bhramayan sarva-bhutani yantrarudhani mayaya*
> <div align="right">(<i>BG</i>, 18:61)</div>
>
> *Ishvarah*, the Supreme Lord, dwells in the hearts of all living beings, making all beings move with his *maya* (power).
>
> - The mere knowing of a principle is not the same as realizing it. An aspirant needs to realize the Lord.

The divine is the inner dweller in everyone's heart. We are all embraced in its support. This calls for us to open our eyes to the unity amongst all, as we all have the same source and the same enabler.

What exists is a shared humanity with its apparent variance but deep underlying sameness.

But equally, knowing is different from surrendering. Having known, when we live in surrender to the unity, we live beyond all boundaries.

Beyond Boundaries

Why do we lock our homes when we go on vacation? Isn't an unoccupied house most susceptible to theft? But what about when the owner of the house resides fully in it? Can the house be thieved as easily then?

As we interact with others and negotiate our relationships, what kind of boundary can serve our purpose? Should building boundaries be about locking doors and erecting walls that the other cannot cross? Or can the alternative be to abide fully in ourselves instead? For seamlessly seated in full abidance, can anyone thieve us?

The debate definitely shifts. Abiding in the Self is the safe ground from which we begin to first find our confidence and rid ourselves of the fear of being thieved, and only then allow ourselves to expand beyond our vulnerabilities and self-created boundaries into unity.

A deliverance from the illusion of separation is a deliverance from boundaries. It is about being more seated in ourselves, and from that space of inner fullness, moving fearlessly beyond boundaries to bonding. Every moment of life is about interdependence and togetherness. It is knowing that the source of all is the same, and the source manifests in various forms which are interdependent.

Our lives and our growth need the 'other'. It is true that it takes two to tango. Bob Dylan was right when he sang, 'Everybody serves somebody.'

What lies beyond boundaries is life itself. The very moment of birth dawns with a pair of extended hands bringing us into this world. Even death is a service – we need the other to serve us so that we can die with dignity – put on the funeral pyre, we move into dusk too, served by a pair of extended hands. Where can the boundary line possibly lie?

15

Dewdrops of Forgiveness

'When for a tumbler of water, a fistful of salt becomes too bitter to hold, the only option before it, is to become the ocean,' says the Buddhist monk Thich Nhat Hanh, in his mellow and compassionate voice.

True, but difficult, yet inescapable. Herein lies the journey of forgiveness —a journey to our own expansion.

For me, forgiveness has been my challenge, my growth and my prayer. I pray that in forgiving, I may receive the blessing of forgiveness itself.

Forgiveness as an Inspired Choice

No day ends without us having forgiven. The ant that crawls along my kitchen floor, my dog who spills my tea with his wagging tail, my friend who gets me delayed or speaks hurtful words, a family member who does not keep a promise, are all forgiven against the backdrop of love. Forgiveness flows easily when the underlying love and commitment allows us to overlook and forget all acts of omission. Therein lies a generosity that seeks the goodness in the other, rather than judging them.

But what happens when the foundations of love and commitment themselves are under attack? The real journey of forgiveness begins then.

When people behave unlovingly and hurt us, forgiveness warrants reconciliation, and reconciliation bases itself on an apology. Forgiving someone when they acknowledge their mistake and apologize becomes an act of generosity, and the apology makes forgiving easier. Honesty and integrity are the catalysts of the happy trio of mutual ownership, repentance and forgiveness.

But the challenge of forgiveness is most apparent when no apology is forthcoming, for then forgiveness remains but a partial act. The only recourse left then is a decision to step out of scarcity and seize the essence of life and living. It is to forgive with no reservations because inherently it is motivated by a decision to take care of ourselves. It's a gift we give ourselves – of stepping out of the agony of waiting for an apology.

We navigate life by laid out conventions, but sometimes we can also navigate by abandoning those very conventions. The burden of our self-esteem, our ego-driven public image, is like the Vietnamese bikes of burden which need constant balancing. Forgiveness is putting these down and letting go the heavy block of burden we had chosen to carry up until now. To be hurt by somebody's action is painful, but to hold on to that pain becomes our suffering.

The decision to carry the burden was of our own choosing and putting it down is our decision – and the resulting peace our own relief. It is releasing ourselves from our self-imposed exile as we stand freed from the prison walls of anger, frustration, resentment and blame. Replaying, retelling and relishing our wounds begets more trauma as our psyche gets stuck there. Trapped in this prison, the body and the mind can adapt many times but it is impossible to adapt forever without succumbing to suffering.

Yet, forgiveness does require deep work. It demands of us the understanding of the wound and the experience itself. It requires the courage to go back to our own Auschwitz. In a strange way, eliminating the hurt draws us closer to its base. In revisiting the source of our pain, our hurt throbs afresh and in that rawness, we begin to reconfigure our relationship to it. Forgiveness may not arise from our broken parts, but it arises through the broken parts, which as they begin to heal become the 'whole' in us. This is where the story of forgiveness is written in words of compassion. We rewrite our grievance story. We write one that is larger than the story that had left us hurt and robbed.

The rewritten story is one of finding our inner North Star and coming into our own strength and our humanity. It becomes the freedom to experience opinions, ideas and perspectives without the edges of judgement. It is to widen our perspectives, temper our expectations and commit to our happiness in light of realigned hopes and wishes. Forgiveness is a promise to preserve the light-heartedness of the heart. The expansion of the tumbler into the ocean begins at this point of integration.

It is stepping out of the karmic cycle itself. Although the wheel of karma will unfold its effects on all, in forgiving we cease to add any new karma and thereby step out of it. Acceptance of 'what is' frees us from attachment to what 'should be'. We change our grudge list to a wish list. It is the release of all stuck energy which can then begin to flow seamlessly. Forgiveness is an expansion through losses, that allows for gain even in the loss.

It is a point of expansion in which all lie encompassed. Forgiveness then takes on the quality of surrender. As Lord Krishna indicates, forgiveness is itself a divine quality and its source is the divine itself:

> *tejah kshama dhritih shaucham adroho nati-manita*
> *bhavanti sampadam daivim abhijatasya bharata II*
> *(BG, 16:3)*
>
> Amongst other qualities, forgiveness appears in one who is high born in divine wealth.

> *budhir jnanam asammohah kshama satyam damah shamah*
> *sukham duhkham bhavo bhayam chabhayameva cha*
> *(BG, 10:4)*
>
> From me alone arises the intellect, knowledge, clarity, forgiveness, truthfulness, sense control, joy and sorrow, birth and death, fear and reassurance.

- The soft ground of forgiveness arises not through an act of will, but from the inspiration that arises within us as we surrender to the Truth. The source of this inspiration is our expansion towards our own inner reality and higher Self.
- It is not that we decide to forgive and then surrender. It is from the very surrendering that the fragrance of forgiveness arises.

Forgiveness as a Way of Being

Forgiveness then becomes the gift of being in the present moment. In the present moment, there is no hurt because each moment is unblemished and innocent. The Buddha said that there is nothing to forgive because 'I don't know yesterday, I only know today.' Forgiveness is meeting everyone as if it was the first time we are meeting them – in their full innocence.

Instead of barbed fences around the line of control, forgiveness then builds the ground to plant saplings of hope along the line of peace. It is the recognition of the fact that to hurt and be hurt presumes love. Whatever our actions be, they are either an act of love or a search for it. In that love, it is about reminding ourselves of the good in the other. The axe cuts down the sandalwood tree, but the fragrant sandalwood imparts its perfume to the very axe that cuts it.

Is forgiveness an act, an attitude or a virtue? As I experience it, beyond all notions, forgiveness is like a dewdrop. One which has passed through the bitter cold of the winter night to arrive as a fragile dot of freshness in the new dawn, and spreading its freshness, dissipates into the earth becoming nothing, or perhaps everything.

16

Thanksgiving

Temples and worship have been part of the Indian ethos. As a child, I remember the joy at the prospect of getting sweet *prasada* for going to the temple – probably the only draw at that age. However, today when temples have been shut due to COVID, I find myself wondering about these rituals.

Temple closure notwithstanding, my spiritual teacher had initiated me into a practice called *manas puja* (mental worship). In this form of worship, we mentally organize the offering, offer it while praying and return with our prasada. Doing this mental ritual over a period of time brought the dynamics of my 'offering' and 'receiving' to the forefront of my mind. It took away the busyness of preparing the offering, and instead brought focus to its source.

What we offer to the Lord is *naivedyam,* and what we get back is prasada. What continues to strike me and humble me is the realization that no matter what I choose to offer – the objects of offering, the inspiration to offer and the opportunity to offer all come from a source beyond me. I am not the creator of anything I offer – I simply gather the offerings together. Then, in return for the simple act of offering, I am blessed with prasada.

I begin to realize my insignificance in the scheme of things and equally a deep gratitude develops for the grand ceremony of life of which I have the privilege of being a part. In the flow of giving and receiving, I stand as a beneficiary of both.

This births reflection on giving, receiving and the notion of gratitude thereof. Yes, it is true that gratitude should be cultivated as it begets happiness, yet I wonder why humans struggle so much with it? The attitude of gratitude warrants some unravelling.

Gratitude in Otherness

India is a land of mixed fortunes. We see humongous wealth and abject poverty in parallel gaze as the slums nestle with mansions. The notion of gratitude that is often touted is to look at the less fortunate and feel grateful for one's blessings.

I have often pondered the absurdity of having a sense of gratitude in comparison to the deprivation of others. But what about counting my own blessings? Yes, I should count my blessings, but the counting is best done outside the context of others. Others' deprivation and my blessings seen under the lens of otherness are two sides of the same coin.

Gratitude is counting my own blessings. It is to see how life has laid out its gifts for me and for my purpose. The comparison with others becomes groundless.

Naivedyam – An Offering in Oneness

Can gratitude develop in the space of separateness? The giving and taking are the actions, yet the effect will be very different based on the attitude with which they are done.

Is there really a giver or taker? If I give with a sense of being a giver while making the other feel obliged that they are takers, what I end up doing is creating a subject–object relationship. This subject–object contract creates duality and breeds separateness. In the space of separateness, gratitude is difficult to cultivate.

We see this play out so often between parents and children, between spouses or even friends, which furthers the divide between the individuals. Unfortunately, every time this is done, both lose. The other person's isolation increases and in this space of isolation, gratitude does not blossom.

The rhythm of giving and taking has to be set out of 'oneness' and not otherness. Giving without a sense of 'doer-ship', or shall I say 'giver-ship', elicits gratitude.

Taking another look at our vocabulary may offer the solution as we substitute the word 'giving' with the word 'offering'. It is apparent that that there is a clear and reciprocal relationship between 'offering' and gratitude. In the Bhagavad Gita, Lord Krishna clearly shows us this direction:

> *yat tu pratyupakaratham phalam uddisya va punah*
> *diyate ca pariklistam tad danam rajas am smrtam II*
> (*BG*, 17:21)
>
> That which is given with purpose of gaining a return, aiming at a reward or given with reluctance, that giving is said to be in the mode of passion.

- The 'giving' has to be done from the heart with expecting nothing in return. If given with expectation of some return or favour, or done grudgingly, then giving is in the mode of mere *rajas* (passion). That giving is not an offering; instead, it is impure and creates a divide – making it a gift of darkness.
- But when the giving is from the heart and in oneness, it becomes an offering. And an offering evokes gratitude.
- What is also apparent is that if the giving is done from love, then what is offered – the object – ceases to matter. What matters is the togetherness and appreciation that is shared. Given with a spirit of offering, even the smallest token is gratefully accepted.

Prasada – A Gift of Value

Gratitude is recognizing the value of the gift – what is given and what has always been there. But can a gift have any value if it is not fully received? Prasada is receiving the gift.

It is recognizing the everlasting. And the everlasting is revealed only to those who seek it, those who know that the door to the invisible must be visible. In René Daumal's book, *Mount Analogue*, the mountain stood revealed only to those who honestly sought it.

This has been the promise of Lord Krishna too:

*tesham satata-yuktanam bhajatam priti-purvakam
dadami buddhi-yogam tam yena mam upayanti te II*

(*BG*, 10:10)

To those who seek me in loving devotion, I give them the knowledge by which they can attain me.

What I offer to the Lord is myself – my best and my worst. What I get in return is the prasada of purity, bliss, joy and peace, no matter what the situation in my life. Prasada is the understanding of reality.

Life unfolds in multiple ways; not all events are pleasant. It may be difficult to be grateful for a loved one's death or betrayal and loss. Gratitude is not for what we get or lose; it is for the moment that dawns. Each moment is a moment of opportunity impregnated with possibilities. It unfolds as an opportunity for me to school my doubts, simplify my faith and trust the possibilities of growth that lie in every event of my life. This is the value of the gift.

Everything that makes more of me than I have ever been, makes me grateful. When the happy and unhappy events of life unfold, for both I am grateful. I am grateful that life still remembers me and holds me. It gives me an opportunity to set in place that which was already in me and draws me to what is greater yet. The blessings are an opportunity for joy and abundance, while the challenges are an opportunity for growth. Everything serves with purpose.

My gratitude for each moment.

Gratitude in Oneness

Gratitude is an acknowledgement of oneness and all that stems from it. It is recognizing that naivedyam and prasada in their material and non-material constructs come from the same source. Giving and receiving are but one act, for we receive when we give.

It is impossible to be grateful and negative at the same time. Appreciating and acknowledging the presence of others as a life form is gratitude. Expressed in acts of giving and receiving, what blossoms is love.

Gratitude is the very acknowledgement of life and the privilege of living it. It is about being part of the world and letting it be part of us along with all its conveniences and inconveniences. It is a quiet honouring of all that is. Gratitude is not a postscript. It is living life in thanksgiving while sitting in the temple of life itself.

THREE

Turnings of Joy

Abiding in the Self

17

A Meeting with Faith

It was nine years ago. I had been in conversation with a very successful corporate leader, trying to model his success. While success is a grand outer manifestation, my effort was to understand the deeper structures that lie behind success.

In trying to assess his core beliefs, I asked him if all his beliefs were taken away and he was left with but one, what would that belief be?

He answered, 'My belief in God.'

He smiled at the surprise on my face, and asked if I knew God. When I answered in the negative, he said, 'I am sure you know God. Think of the times when you have experienced God.'

This statement has stayed with me through the years. Today, as I look over the years of my life, I recognize the numerous ways in which I have experienced a higher power. While the experiences and circumstances have been many and of various hues, the standout experience has been of engendered faith which today enriches my life. What I express in the lines that follow are its different shades.

Call it God, call it Divinity, call it Spirit ... once I place my faith in this strength, can I ever be weak?

Faith in Difficult Times

There are some phases of our lives that march in, determined to challenge us. For me this was my thirties, when caught between the demands of being a young parent and the sudden and critical medical needs of my father as he battled cancer, I found myself plated out as the classic sandwich generation.

Parenthood is a time of great reckoning, for we are asked to shoulder a responsibility for which we are mostly untrained. My journey as a young mother took me on this path. I found myself negotiating my way with great fervour, but scant understanding. My firstborn, my son, gave me the opportunity to negotiate the challenges of his adolescent years, individual idiosyncrasies, medical necessities, the fire of youth. This, along with my own need to have a perfect solution at each turn, had me baffled and somewhat overwhelmed. Meanwhile, as I looked at my younger one, my daughter, I struggled with the knowing that she too needed the time and attention that was her right.

When challenges present themselves, rough are their edges but deep their meaning. It was in these times I realized that faith means opening up to challenges and navigating them. It becomes a knowing that the problem and the solution both lie within us. Effected by truth, faith calls for us to grow into our solutions.

While solutions are need-based and require customization, the first port of call is the understanding that we have a tendency to impute our frailties to life. In doing so, the lack of faith in oneself and in the goodness of life exhibits as blame, helplessness, doubt, and other crutches.

The way out is knowing that a space can be but once occupied. Faith and lack of faith cannot coexist in the same space. Faith becomes the removal of all doubt. It is the ground where answers begin to emerge based on better understanding and well-grounded hope. It is to know that life presents us with trials, limitations and uncertainties, and yet it is knowing that limitations have their limits and uncertainties their certainty. Albert Einstein said, 'As far as the laws of mathematics refer to reality, they are not certain; as far as they are certain, they do not refer to reality.'

A determined effort to work with my son to help him discover his strengths entailed bringing about a shift in his mindset and expanding his skill set. Academic skills, life skills and social skills – he grew better at them all. American writer and artist Henry Miller was right when he said, 'Destiny is what you are supposed to do in life. Fate is what kicks you in the ass to make you do it.' This was faith at work; for faith is knowing that fate is the runway on which we will take-off towards our destiny.

For me, seeing my son emerge as a confident young man who can handle the pulls of life with a calm and ordered mind and an open heart, has been a living testimony of my belief in cause and effect. As we sow, so shall we reap. A law that self-administers. Faith is placing our belief in this law, which is unmistakably universal.

For my son, faith became a way of knowing that we please nobody by becoming somebody. It is to know that ultimately, we will rise to the level of our source. And in that journey, faith is knowing that the feet will find their ground and the eyes will find their seeing in the light.

For both of us, faith became a way of seeing that through the challenges and in the easy being denied to us, what was being offered was a gift instead – a gift of greater knowing and higher being. It is true what Maya Angelou said, 'Faith is knowing there is a rainbow in the cloud.'

Meanwhile, for my father, as he was cared for and supported, faith became knowing that the touchpoints of support are always there. Sadly, as he moved on, for all of us, faith became the acceptance that a shorter term of life is also long if it has been lived well.

By my mid-thirties, I had come to know, and know deeply, that faith is postponing oneself to something higher, knowing that it will be indescribable and invaluable.

Faith in Good Times

With many trials resolved, yet knowing that more may come, I look at my life and realize that faith is the way in which we hold the conversation of our life. The way we converse, are the conversations we hear. Lord Krishna distills it further:

> *sattvanurupa sarvasya shraddha bhavanti bharata*
> *shraddha-mayo ')yam purusho yo yach-chhraddhah sa eva sah* ||
> (*BG*, 17:3)
>
> The faith of all humans conforms to the nature of their minds. All people possess faith; whatever the nature of their faith, that is verily what they are.
>
> - *Shraddha* (faith) is understanding-based conviction.
> - Based on our understanding we place our faith. Where we place it and what we believe in, shapes the direction of our lives.
> - The type of faith a human being has is in accordance with his natural disposition. Some have faith in doing what is good; others in doing what is needed for fulfilling their desires; while others become victims of blind faith.

It becomes apparent that what seems like the manufacturing of will, comes from its unmanufactured better half: faith.

But it is important to know that true faith does not weigh one down. It can only up-end. It runs the runner and lights the light.

Today for me, faith is the space replete with trust in which I stand together with my son. I sense him stand behind me watching my back, while I look out for him with my own backward gaze, both of us knowing that the other is already blessed and protected. Faith is twice blessed.

Faith in All Times

Woven into the fabric of my life, faith has become the strength of every thread as the warp and weft interweave. Faith lies in seeing the invisible in the visible; the strength of a seed as it erupts from the ground, as also seeing the visible in the invisible – the omnipresence of every atom itself.

As I know it now, faith is understanding that life is inherently simple and easy, and the laws of nature are naturally followed. It is trusting our knowing as much as trusting the way life expresses itself. In both, it is accepting the seat of the divine in us.

Faith is that container that allows for grace to descend. It is the knowing of what I might call God. When I kneel down and pray, wanting to ascend, doesn't grace too descend? Such is the calling of faith.

In its full expanse, faith is the essential and wilful surrender for our necessitated liberty. It is imperative that faith and liberty meet. This has now become my core belief, the ground upon which stands the pillar of success.

*A deep silence revives the listening
and the speaking of those two
who meet on the riverbank.*

*Like the ground turning green in a spring wind
Like the birdsong beginning inside the egg*

*Like this universe coming into existence,
the lover wakes and whirls
in a dancing joy,*

*then kneels down
in praise.*

(Coleman Barks, 'Birdsong From
Inside the Egg', *The Essential Rumi*)

18

The Wealth of Beauty

Today is the Blood Moon day – a phenomenon where the moon will be closest to the Earth in its orbit. Maybe it's natural for the moon to draw my attention, as it does in almost all mystical traditions. In Vedic vocabulary, *Soma* is synonymous with the moon and stands for all that is beautiful. It evokes a soft delight, and is related to the purity of mind, which then finds beauty in the world and comes to know it.

The draw of beauty is but natural. We are not just drab creatures of bone and flesh but creatures that rejoice in the richness of life, for what we see outside, in essence, is our own richness. What we wish to see outside is what lies inherently within us. The natural corollary being, in denying beauty outside we deny its presence within us.

So subjective is the notion of beauty, yet so enthralling its effect. Why do we want our hair to be in place and our clothes to sit right? Why do we decorate our homes? Why do we have such high appreciation for art and music? Why does natural beauty captivate us? Isn't the entire gamut of aesthetics in our life nothing but a call of beauty?

Today, I contemplate the ways in which I have beheld such beauty and the way I see it expressed in our life and living.

The Beauty of the Moment

The moment in which beauty is beheld is magical. Many a time, beauty seems to herald its arrival with an exclamation, a sense of awe, a placeholder for the unknown that comes to sudden knowing. It is the moment an infant breaks into a smile, or when walking along a path, a crimson rose suddenly springs into vision, making its presence felt. In awe, I see the fleeting moments of beauty.

Equally, beauty also lies in enduring moments where the full expression of life is experienced. The more I see the young, the more I admire their stamina and strength; but the more I see the old, the more I admire the strength that holds up the failing stamina. It lies in the perfection of seeing the variations and imperfections of this world. It is in the perfect gleam of a glazed cup and it is in the cracks of an ageing kettle. A Kintsugi and Wabi-sabi of sorts. I suppose, the beauty of what is expressed far exceeds the beauty of the expression.

But what are the other facets of beauty besides just the moment? Beyond the glimpse of the moment is there anything else staring back at us?

Beauty of the Form

There is equal beauty in the bonsai as there is beauty in the banyan tree. Yet, what really is the profile of beauty?

In the Yoga Sutra, Sage Patanjali uses the term *kaya sampat*, to describe the bodily wealth inherent in our form. The four major categories that comprise kaya sampat are: *rupa* (beauty), *bala* (vigour and vitality), *vajra* (indestructability) and *lavanya* (charm).

Rupa is the beauty of the external lines of the form, its appearance. It is the beauty our form expresses in different stages of our life.

Why does appearance attract? Is it because beauty lies in agreeable forms – the sharp definition of a beautiful face, a chiselled body and flawless skin? True, but ask a portrait painter and they will tell you that atrophied by age and pulled by tension on our faces, it is the asymmetry that becomes agreeable and lends intrigue and beauty to form.

Bala is the beauty that lies in the strength of the form. The structure and design that supports the form and gives it stronger definition.

I see it all around me. The structure of the aeroplane, of the bird, the beast and the human, all support the form and enhance the beauty. But equally, beauty also lies in the design that supports the structure. The beauty of a perfect form is that it screams for attention, whilst the beauty of a perfect design is that it rarely calls for it. The bilateral symmetry of the physical structure lends beauty to the human form.

Vajra is our innate indestructibility that allows form to hold out through all eventualities. It is the aspect of beauty that gives us resilience, robustness and glow.

After all, the luster of our hair lies in the roots and the flavour of the fruit lies in the health of the tree that has weathered all seasons.

And yet, isn't there still something else about beauty that mesmerizes us?

That mesmerizing pull lies in *lavanya*, the quality of tastefulness. It is the charm and elegance that so delights us – be it in a person, object or place. It is the seamlessness and ease that attracts. It is the charisma of a silver screen idol – the X factor. Isn't it also the beauty of a white rose drawn on white paper, merging and yet standing apart? Light etches of charcoal smoothening themselves into ease. A simplicity and lightness which attracts.

Such is the beauty of the form. More than in the obvious, it lies in the folds.

Beauty of the Spirit

On looking deeper, I realize that beauty lies in the equation with the Self. The hidden layers of beauty are also in the union of what presents itself outside with what it invokes inside as pleasure and pain. The pride in a father's eyes and the drooling wag of a dog, all invite an embrace and joy. And yet, beauty also lies in the soft and painful cry of the heart. The pain of the caterpillar before it becomes a butterfly. And what about the pain of the tide as it sees the child resolutely swimming against its stride?

Equally, beauty lies in completeness. We are not just in our form, nor just in our sensations and thoughts. We are but a composite of form and spirit. For as Cicero, a great Roman orator, said, 'I admire a young man who has something of the old in him, so do I an old one who has something of a young man.' Beauty is complete.

Above all, beauty is essence. It is elegance, and as much the sweetness of sugar as it is the taste of water. As Lord Krishna says:

> *raso humapsu kaunteya prabhasmi shashi-surayoh*
> *pranavah sarva-vedeshu shabdah khe paurusham nrishu*
>
> *(BG, 7:8)*
>
> I am the taste in water, the radiance of the sun and the moon. I am the sacred syllable Om. I am the sound in ether, and the ability in humans.
>
> - Beauty lies in knowing the essence behind all manifestation. That essence is nothing but the divine.
> - Here Lord Krishna says that He himself is the essence of water. This essence is what gives water its sapidity, which in turn leads to the manifestation of all tastes.

Celebrating beauty in the tapestry of our life is joyful, for it allows us to touch the beauty within. The greater the variation, the richer the tapestry – the source of all being the divine itself. This is the wealth of beauty, its truth.

Tonight, as I continue to look at the moon, I reckon that beauty is the vocabulary in which form converses with spirit. Beauty endures, when in this conversation between the two, it is recognized that behind its greatest glory, the beauty of beauty lies in its truth. And only then, perhaps, under the perfect setting of the moonlight, when dinner is set on the table for two, two are at the table.

O how much more doth beauty beauteous seem,
By that sweet ornament which truth doth give!
The rose looks fair, but fairer we it deem
For that sweet odour which doth in it live...

And so of you, beauteous and lovely youth,
When that shall fade, my verse distills your truth.

(William Shakespeare, 'Sonnet 54')

19

Turnings of Joy

Does the sun shine *on* us or *in* us? Do the stars herald the romance or is the landscape of romance within us?

Thinking about these questions draws my attention to Zadie Smith's essay, 'Find your Beach', which with humour and humility points to our rather compulsive conversations about joy. She points to how, in our times, joy has been made into a commissioned project, something to be chased. But the essential question that remains is: Do we need to undergo pain to feel joy?

Is joy something to be found or does its wellspring lie within us? I wonder, do we need to find our beach, or do we have the capacity to be in a state of 'in beach'?

Clarity

Joy lies on the same line of latitude as do our thoughts and emotions. Moments in our lives when we have been 'in beach' have been moments when the mind is innocent and our nature shines forth without offering any obstructions and doubts. A kind of organic magnetism that draws towards itself what belongs to it.

Where the lines of latitude and longitude meet may be more a function of where they are drawn: outside us or within us. This is the crucial difference between the modern-day quest for happiness from external sources, and the quest of the ancients and sages to find the source of perennial joy within. Joy has been the aspiration for both, the difference being where they looked.

The joy I experience and express is what I intrinsically am.

Joy is not an accidental discovery. Joy is the ecstasy of being, with centred discipline. A state of perennial joy, the state of *vishoka* (sorrowless joy) decidedly pointed out by Sage Vyasa in the *Yoga Sutra*:

> *visoka va jyotismati II*
>
> (*YS*, 1:36)
>
> The state of consciousness which is vishoka (free from sorrow and anguish) and infused with *jyotishmati* (inner light).
>
> - Sage Vyasa firmly asserts that joy is a state free from all sorrow. It is a state of consciousness where we know we exist beyond the confines of our body, senses and mind.

But how shall we access this state of consciousness called vishoka?

As we turn our gaze inwards and begin to explore our inner landscape in a disciplined manner, we begin to know and discern who we really are, our physical and subtle aspects alike. As clarity dawns, we get to know our own mind along with all its aspects that bind and disempower us.

The more our mind watches itself, the more it begins to acknowledge its tedium of tears and erosions of emptiness. Doubts, fears, anger, guilt, grief, regret and shame begin to loosen their hold on us. We can now observe our faltering without being perturbed by them. The blessing is that now our mind ceases to be in the whirl of wanting to lose itself or find itself. Keeping our hands firmly on the helm of our thoughts, self-control becomes our strength and right thought our proficiency.

As the darkness of our mind abates, the light begins to reveal itself. This state of inner luminosity is jyotishmati. A state where the mind begins to look beyond itself at the wonders of the world and the magnificence of the creator of this world. Perhaps the physicist Arthur S. Eddington was in this state when he said, 'Something unknown is doing we don't know what.' This is the blessing of an open and unified mind.

Healing

A calmness begins to descend. Under the luminance of inner clarity, our emotional hurts are healed and traces of sorrow wiped out. We begin to tread lightly while landing heavy.

Joy in its mature state is a space of inner healing and inherent bliss. It is a state where we are able to face ourselves. We acknowledge and accept ourselves in as much as we do others. James Allen, the British philosophical writer and poet, was on point when he said, 'A man becomes calm in the measure that he understands himself as a thought-evolved being.'

From this space of healing, we see that the world is not the source of our sorrow, and we give up the need to detach ourselves from it. Such a unified mind becomes the point of landing where perennial joy itself becomes our locus – it is wherever we are. Our mind now rides the waves of joy. Not outside us but within us is the joy we were seeking.

Once healed, we have the power to heal. We find ourselves more integrated and in unison with the world. The world and our relationship with it become reflections of our own inherent joy. This is where our joy finds itself manifested. For what joy is there in us if it can't find measure in the joy we bring to our loved ones?

Essence

'The greater the conscious effort, the less the subconscious response,' stated Émile Coué, the French psychologist, when he defined the law of reversed effort.

The more we try to float, the more we sink; the more we try to sink, the more we float. The more we seek joy, the less we will find it.

Resolution comes through the assertion of eastern philosophy – joy is our essential nature. All we have to do is to step back, move out of our own way and allow our joy to bubble forth.

Isn't this what I experience when, in her own soft and fragrant ripeness, my daughter feels the impulse to mother me? That moment when she insists that I press my eyeliner a bit longer for a sharper definition; the space that is held between us as the young one lingers that extra moment over a coffee and croissant. In that moment, what I see is an untethered soul. And that moment begins to hold everything in essence, replete with togetherness and love.

Equally, isn't there joy in the smell of freshly baked bread, crusty in its freshness and unscented in its fragrance? It is the purity of essence and what radiates from it.

Joy is seeing the warp and the weft in a cloth draped plainly. It is the axis. Or what T.S. Eliot called 'the still point of the turning world'.

Surrender

There comes a time in our development when in giving up beliefs for faith and trust we ease into a state of joy. The moment of reckoning is when our mind begins to recognize that we can give only what we have received.

The joyous mind is one that recognizes the alchemy of nature and nurture. It recognizes the nurturance it has received in every unfoldment of life, and thereby feels complete. As the poet Rilke said, 'Wind consoles and fire is consolation.' This is when one answer meets all questions.

In its full manifestation, joy is the blossoming of the bud as it reaches towards the sunlight and spreads its fragrance, knowing that one day it will pendant from the very same branch. Joy is a total and fearless immersion in the conversation of life, exhibiting itself as essence.

Joy is this very moment of writing these words and becoming the written. It is a moment of surrender – when all understanding becomes understood.

And then, joy is living forever 'in beach' and living joyfully even amongst the joyless. It is to live in a state where the human and divine in us meet – a state of turning – that lies within us.

*The secret turning in us
makes the universe turn.
Head unaware of feet,
and feet head. Neither cares.
They keep turning ...*

*I stand up, and this one of me
turns into a hundred of me.
They say I circle around you.
Nonsense. I circle around me ...*

*Dance when you are broken open.
Dance, if you've torn the bandage off.
Dance in the middle of the fighting.
Dance in your blood.
Dance when you are perfectly free.*

(Coleman Barks, 'The Turn:
Dance in your blood', *The Essential Rumi*)

20

The Calling of Love

The calling of love will always remain. Our birth is love itself. Its abundance is etched in our memory as it is our first deep experience.

A friend of mine has been on a quest to understand love. He once took on a project of making a movie on what love is. At the Jaipur Literary Festival, he interviewed numerous literary minds. He got many answers but failed to arrive at a conclusion. The difficulties in answering his query seemed apparent.

Today as I ponder this question, the one thing that seems clear is that love is an all-encompassing phenomenon, and so naturally, it is impossible to describe the whole. One can begin the exploration by looking at its parts but it must be remembered that the whole is always greater than the sum of its parts. Therein lies the difficulty.

Over the last few years, love has become my greatest inquiry. Seeing challenging relationships all around me led me to question the very word, yet in my heart I felt the need to know it and hopefully come to a point where I can 'be love' itself. Standing at our shrine in Khajuraho, I remember urging my spiritual teacher to help me understand love. He simply smiled and said, 'Know that you already have begun to understand it.' So, in all humility and reverence, I pen down my thoughts on love.

Falling in Love – The Romanticism of Love

The romanticism of love has been carefully cultivated by seeing only the lighter side of it. But incessant holding on makes even the light seem heavy. Hold a sheet of paper or even a single thought for a long time and it begins to weigh us down. The hand hurts and the mind tires. On the other hand, while holding the heavy may be difficult, it would be exactly the right reason to do so. Love is to be held with all its weight.

It's true that love is passion. There is no love without the touch of passion – even a thread needs the touch of the needle to stitch. But I wonder if passion is human enough? Why else would its root be suffering? When love becomes a compelling desire, in holding on tightly to it we strangle its very flow and feel suffocated in the bargain. Being weighed down, does it become a rut – mere virility and muliebrity?

In the Gita, often called the 'Song of Love', Lord Krishna clarifies that:

> *ye hi sansparsha-ja bhoga duhkha-yonaya eva te*
> *adyantavantah kaunteya na teshu ramate budhah II*
> (*BG*, 5:22)
>
> The pleasures that arise from contact with the sense objects, though appearing as enjoyable, are verily a cause of sorrow; they have a beginning and an end. A wise man does not delight in them.

- The reason sensual pleasures give only momentary gratification is because the senses are themselves limited and the objects are not permanent.
- The constantly changing nature of objects and the sense of loss that this produces leads to anger, grief and anxiety.
- Love, if objectified, would face the same consequences. The 'falling in love' becomes a falling into the anxiety of love.

The conventions of love are aplenty. They keep up the buoyancy of love. But many in their unknowing are determined to escape the conventions. They do so only to fall into the clutches of an obvious but more damaging conventional solution – and an impersonal one at that – where commitment is forsaken for freedom.

So how shall we love?

Thich Nhat Hanh is right when he says, 'To love without knowing how to love, wounds the person we love.' The 'how to' of love needs us to distinguish clearly between two kinds of love – one is the grasping, mean and egotistical kind of love which cripples, while the other is one that stems from all that is good in each of us and lends to the expansion of all.

Seeing that Love is 'All'

Space is all. Inside and outside, both are in space itself. Isn't love space?

Love is 'all'. It is everything we may see it to be. It is also what we see it as not. And, in fact, it is also what we simply miss seeing.

What we see it to 'be' – The spectrum of love

Love is erroneously stereotyped as romantic love, but don't we also love our parents, siblings, children, friends and neighbours? This brings us to the point that love is a spectrum.

The colours of the spectrum of love have already been paint-brushed by the Greeks as:

- Eros: Burning passion
- Philia: Shared brotherly goodwill
- Ludus: Playful love
- Pragma: Love with commitment that requires understanding and compromise
- Agape: Selfless and compassionate love with no expectations
- Philautia: Embracing ourselves fully and then only being able to embrace others
- Storge: Unwavering devotion, a love that knows forgiveness, acceptance, and sacrifice. Storge does not waver.

Love is a gamut. Love is not any one but love is all of the above. We experience all the above dimensions of love at different times, in different places and with different people. In fact, we may be experiencing them at the same time for different people.

Interestingly, igniting any one kind of love starts to give us a clue to the others. For instance, eros without ludus may become boring, and eros without philia may become exploitative. Love itself matures. Given enough time, even eros matures into storge in married couples.

What we see it as 'not' – Love thy enemy

'Darkness cannot drive out darkness; only light can do that. Hate cannot drive out hate, only love can do that.' The words of Martin Luther King Jr. have echoed through the ages.

Love is a necessitated expansion. Loving thy enemy is love – an expansive process. Our enemy, if we permit them to, unwittingly moves us towards our own expansion.

Even in loving our enemies what we are taught is to accommodate the other side of the polarity – our own intolerance, dislike and hate. A possible purpose it might serve is to prompt us to grow such that we learn to hold the negativity coming in from our enemy. Shutting out is easier and less challenging than holding space for the negative. It becomes our call for compassion – an expansion.

A Jungian perspective on the same could be that: you've got what you spot. Spotting the negative in our enemy may prompt us to look within and allow us to embrace our darker side, our shadow – an expansion. Maybe our lovelessness is nothing but our own fears and shadows, our own incongruity which clouds our love.

On a lighter note, even when you hate your enemy and gossip about them, you are including them because you are dependent on them to make yourself feel good. The non-circles are good for the ego of the circle. But in including the non-circle, the circle itself has expanded!

What we 'miss' seeing – The lover in the scientist

Love perhaps is universal. Let's take Newton's Third Law of Motion: For every action there is an equal and opposite reaction. For me, the point of focus is the word 'every'. What happens and how we name the happening is not the point here – the point is that it happens to everyone, to all!

Even Einstein claimed, 'Either everything has an explanation or then all is a miracle.' Touching upon the 'all' becomes a matter of transcendence. And love is precisely this – the transcendence of the Self and coming in touch with All. Science in its endeavour to quantify, slices reality, yet it seems it keeps touching the core – universality.

You can't have a wave that is either all trough and no peak, nor the other way around either. A wave essentially is both the peak and trough. The peak is love expressed while the trough is love repressed. But both are love.

The Hard Work of Love

The journey of love is one of going through the sliding doors of our perceptions. Love is a shift of perspective, a changed lens through which we look. It is recognizing and releasing our own thought patterns and stickiness – the hard work of love.

Love can be moments of frustration. But the frustration emerges from our desire to exchange our incomprehension of the other with contempt and rejection. While the latter are ways of engaging with the unwanted, staying with the incomprehension may be the way to unravel the puzzle.

While we believe that the pieces of the puzzle lie outside us, we fail to recognize that we are the pieces of our own puzzle. What we find lacking in the other is what lies blocked in us. The poet Rumi draws our attention by saying, 'Your task is not to seek for love, but merely to seek and find all the barriers within yourself that you have built against it.'

Love is a private affair and not a public matter. Love brings us in touch with our humanity and its failings. When these are unconsciously projected onto the other, they become the blocks to love. Managing these is a private affair and must be done. Or else, lost in public display, love stands forsaken.

Love is apprenticeship. It is not that love grows in skill and strength, but we grow in those through love. Love is the opportunity for growth. It is the invitation to becoming whole. The abandon and togetherness of love is the gift of this inner growth and not a guarantee of love. A sentiment that Alain de Botton, the Swiss-born British philosopher in his book *The Course of Love* has rightly expressed, 'Compatibility is an achievement of love; it must not be its precondition'. For what togetherness can there be between half-broken things? The demands of love are hard, and in the beginning, we are ill-suited to them.

Love is security. Anyone who has love need not worry about losing it. It's better to lose yourself in love than worry about its loss. 'And don't worry about losing. If it is right, it happens – The main thing is not to hurry. Nothing good gets away,' said John Steinbeck.

The hard work of love purposes itself; it makes love easy.

Rising in Love

An aspect of the Gita that never fails to move me is when Arjuna asks Lord Krishna to reveal his true self to him. This was the true call of love – a longing to see the beloved in his full grandeur. Arjuna wished to see Lord Krishna as Lord Krishna was – the omnipotent, omniscient and omnipresent being.

To accept this invitation and enable Arjuna to see the grand vision was a testament of Lord Krishna's love for him in turn. Love is an invitation to see the greatness in the other. But how are we to master this seeing?

Lord Krishna answers by directing us towards devotion:

> *bhaktya tv ananyaya shakya aham evam-vidho 'rjuna*
> *jnatum drashtum cha tattvena praveshtum cha parantapa II*
> (*BG*, 11:54)
>
> Arjuna, through devotion alone, directed towards who I really am, can I be known as I am and entered.

Love is knowing the essence of the other. The 'I' that Lord Krishna refers to is the essence, the truth of us. This is possible only when we are free of negative attachments and animosity.

In reaching out for the truth we come to realize that in essence we are all one – we all are the reflection of the same reality.

Love is devotion, a surrender, a merging. It is a decision to stop resisting and start yielding.

The shifting equations of mature love may not be in our current experience. The new equations begin to get defined with the process of personal unfolding. Having gone through the uncertainties and various disguises, with greater purity we come to abide in our truest nature and become more of human beings. The new equation will no longer be between man and woman but between two humans, each welcoming the other. This is the true labour of love, along with a liberal dose of patience.

Being Love

Love is an allowing, just as the sky allows for rain no matter how much the thunder. Love matures between two human beings who have come to inhabit their humanness. This is what the Greeks knew when they saw the progression of love from eros to storge.

In its full maturity, as beautifully put by Coleman Bark, 'love is like a holiday'. A space of non-judgement, forgiveness and acceptance. Love expresses itself by being it.

My journey of love had gradually brought me to a knowing that the flame of love is lit but by our own light. I thought this would be the highest understanding that was possible to reach. Little did I know that there was more ground to cover. Today, from the space in which I stand, I know that if after all the bashing and chasing is over, if something still remains standing on its own, refusing to be defined, refusing to be diminished and feeling no need to explain itself, then it must be love. In the eternal calling of love, being love is being the lover more than the loved.

Piya Piya karte hamin piya hue, ab piya kisnu khaiye?

Repeating the name of the beloved.
I have become the Beloved myself;
Whom shall I call the Beloved now?

(Bulleh Shah)

21

Partnering with Death

Death is a contemporary of birth. They were both invented in tandem somewhere along the course of history. Batchmates and course-mates, together they graduate to give us our qualifications for Life. In an ever-present horizon of events, what is the role of death? Does it measure our incarnation, or does it partner with it to give it meaning?

It has been exactly a week since I lost my mother-in-law to COVID. Prior to her death, while she was battling COVID in the ICU, the family was quite naturally in the grip of fear and dread. As death became a reality, the flood of sorrow was unleashed. The fear, denial and potential loss had savaged everyone's heart. On hearing the news, the family lapsed into deep sorrow and grief. She was a great presence that had been taken away from us. A period of mourning ensued and somewhere we all began to find some bit of closure. I sat with the tapestry of my feelings and emotions – fear, regret, loss, grief, closure and hope. Each of them deep and significant, yet so varied. This one event has significantly introduced me to my own emotional variance.

Somewhere, I began feeling the need to make sense of death and dying. Is it death or the fear of death that upsets us the most? If death has never been in my experience, how would I really understand it? I have neither died so far, nor conversed with a dead person – all I have seen are dead bodies. And even if I were to be dead, how terrible could I feel about not being there, when I am not there at all? Until I understand death, it will continue to haunt me.

As living beings, our focus is on life the way we understand it. All understanding is bookended between the moment of our birth and the moment of our death. We feel we have understood life as it unfolds between these two ends. But really, is that all there is to life? Is it really just a handspan between birth and death? I wonder if we could benefit by altering the question a bit: Can I build an understanding of life and the possibilities it holds between 'birth and death' as also between 'death and birth'? Isn't this the mysterious zone that few of us comprehend?

Demystifying death is an imperative. Dying needs to be understood with as much clarity as living does. Eastern philosophy throws light on death such that in understanding it, we begin to be free of its fear and willingly incorporate it as part of the spectrum of life. The *Yoga Sutra* explains:

> *Svarasvahi viduso'pi tatharudho'bhinivesah II*
>
> (*YS*, 2:9)
>
> Fear of death carries its own essence and rides (the consciousness) of even the wise.
>
> - The knowledge that death is inevitable and our denial of it is deeply ingrained.

The Fear of Death

As per the world view of the wise, death marks the passage from manifest to un-manifest. It is merely the casting off of the old garment and preparing for the new.

Death really has no power to destroy the essence of life; it remains the same in both birth and death. A rising wave is the manifest form of the same water, which in essence is there even when the wave subsides and becomes un-manifest.

Lack of comprehension of death leads us to fearing it. The fear of dying and clinging to life become two sides of the same coin. And sadly, our life gets dictated by this primal fear.

It goes without saying that we all wish to live for long. All our endeavours when alive are to ensure a long life. This desire to live forever is thwarted at the moment of death. We die against our wishes. We die in regret. All feelings merge into the experience of dying – and this is our final memory.

Sage Vyasa, in his commentaries on the *Yoga Sutra*, clearly expounds that this final memory, the fear of death and clinging to life, creates a subtle pulsation which, in turn, creates a certain atmosphere for our rebirth. This fear houses itself in us in the region of our primitive brain.

Life begins where it had ended. We are reborn, loaded with our past regrets. No wonder our mind clings to life. We realize that death is inevitable, but we also realize that we want to live forever. Thus, we are caught in the grip of fear the moment we are born. And this is the fear we live with.

As we grow and our identification to our body–mind apparatus increases, so does the clinging and fear. We are then in the grip of what Patanjali calls *abhinivesha* (fear of death), an affliction of fear that has us trapped from all sides.

The Pain of Death

Clinging to life makes us resist death. Before we die, we try our best not to die.

Death annihilates everything that was us. We lose all grounds for individuality and autonomy. This loss is very, very painful.

As we grow, death grows with us. If we can grasp this, we may find the strength to live a life where we start releasing our fixation with ourselves. Today I understand that death is nothing but a loss of my own identity, which is my worst possible fear.

When I see this in the general fabric of my life, I begin to realize that I possibly die many times in a single day, every day of my life. Every disappointment, betrayal, failure or loss is a moment of death. Looking at an average lifespan, how many phases of life have we all lived when we died, to be able to live on? The death of the adolescent in me gives birth to the youth in me. Why look so far into the horizon of time? Every time my toast burns or my coffee overspills is a death of sorts. Yet, through the most trivial to the gravest moments, we come forth. What we call human resilience may be nothing more than our deep desire to live on.

Accepting death – its inevitability and essence – begins to change our relationship with death and the loss of those we have loved. For 13 days, the family as per Indian custom, is getting together to mourn the loss of my mother-in-law. But interlaced in the remembrance is the celebration of her life.

I am left wondering, why did we need death to mark her life, to appreciate her and her life? Why do we feel the need for evocative eulogies, when life and its meaning can be celebrated within life itself? But then, would I ever really understand death if I had not known life? Even negation is understood only against the backdrop of the affirmative.

When I look at death either as momentary lapses in my life or as life-altering losses, what does stand out is that maybe it is birth itself which gives us the opportunity to free ourselves from clinging to life. Could this be the real purpose of life? Once again, the *Yoga Sutra* answers in the affirmative:

> *te pratiprasavaheyah suksmah II*
>
> (*YS*, 2:10)
>
> The afflictions are discarded at death only if they have become subtle.
>
> - The afflictions become subtle when their strength and intensity is minimised.
> - This is achieved through ardent practice.

Death and the fear of death come to an end only when we attenuate our afflictions and self-identifications. If not, the vortex of attachment and aversion continues to throw us back into the cycle of death-birth.

The goal of life and any spiritual practice is to minimize and diminish this vortex to a point where it becomes so subtle that it is not the 'content' of the mind anymore.

Living well becomes a powerful way of ensuring a peaceful death, for contentment with life brings readiness for death. A peaceful death becomes the ground for a happy rebirth. A vibrant cycle of life.

Even as I sit and write these words, I do hold an awareness of the fact that simultaneously life is moving in its own rhythm. Every moment, I inhale and exhale almost on autopilot. I notice that my inhalation needs a bit of effort initially but then it becomes smoother and culminates in an effortless exhalation. This effortless exhalation becomes the ground for a more joyful inhalation the next time. And before I know it, I find myself happily nestled in this flow of breath. Within me, I feel life flowing, not bookended by inhalation and exhalation but presencing itself through them.

Swami Vivekananda asserted, 'Saints die and sinners die, kings die and beggars die. They are all going to death and yet this tremendous clinging on to life exists.' The truth is, we all will die, yet the flow of life is far too powerful to be bookended by birth and death.

Death is like turning over the page of a book you are reading, ready to enjoy the next page. Maybe it is from the very stillness at death that all potential of life arises. But then, this stillness at death is the earning of a lifetime itself. Dying is as noble an act as living and deserves its own celebration, a moment of rejoicing. May the heaviness of death forever sit lightly on us.

Peace, my heart, let the time for
the parting be sweet.
Let it not be death but
Completeness.
Let love melt into memory and
Pain into songs.
Let the flight through the sky
End in the folding of wings
Over the nest ...

(Rabindranath Tagore,
'The Gardener LXI: Peace, My Heart')

Leaving My Legacy

We build empires and wish to leave them as a legacy for our descendants. But could that legacy be a mere shadow of ambition coming from an already lived life? While ambition seems forward-looking, legacy seems like looking into the rear-view mirror – going forward, looking backwards.

The draft of legacy we intend to leave behind is meaningfully written with deeply etched grooves of our own understanding, mastery and a sense of claim. While it borrows its pride from this understanding, I wonder if what is worth leaving behind can come from a knowing that steals from the young the opportunities of their own unknowing? Isn't this what makes legacy somewhat a burden for the beneficiary?

> *I had an inheritance from my father,*
> *It was the moon and the sun.*
> *And though I roam all over the world,*
> *The spending of it's never done.*
> (Ernest Hemingway, *For Whom the Bell Tolls*)

Legacy stems from the flow of fulfilled dreams but what about those dreams that are still to be dreamt? Isn't there a certain freedom and romance to dreaming and seeing them come true for yourself? Inherent to the fructification of dreams is the humbling and building of character. Can another understand my dreams without going through my heartbeats of 'un-fulfilment' and achievement?

Legacy is like a half-written contract. It charters the achievements but footnotes the failures – a trap for the unwitting. How would the pool of learning and wisdom grow if not filled with the droplets of one's own tears? The only true legacy is one that leaves behind not the dish but the secret recipe.

And the only secret worth knowing is to know that you exist. You exist for your being and not for your doing. You exist as is. And because you exist, you are the most precious and the most beautiful.

May my legacy be the one that leaves behind the knowing of possibilities, of hope, of hard work, of honesty and of happenstance. Let my life be my legacy. Let this legacy be the gift of a courageous curiosity rather than a conclusive statement. Let it be a studentship of life.

May this legacy live through you and not for you. Let the legacy be of my patiently earned joy. Let that be your inheritance – the abundance that needs neither measure nor mark.

My life has been a quest to abide in my fullness. What I leave for you is not a part of myself but the full of myself. And from that full, even if I were to leave a part, always know that it is full too.

Om Puurnnam-Adah Puurnnam-Idam
Puurnnaat-Puurnnam-Udacyate |
Puurnnasya Puurnnam-Aadaaya
Puurnnam-Eva-Avashissyate ||
Om Shaantih Shaantih Shaantih ||

Om That is Perfect, this is Perfect
Perfection arises from the Perfect
When Perfection is taken from the
Perfect Perfection still remains
Om Peace, Peace, Peace

Peace Invocation
from the *Isavasyopanisad*

Conclusion in continuation…

I am ageless.
I'm every age I have ever been,
I am the ages of all my forefathers as well as my foremothers.

I am ageless.
I am the age of every experience and what it has taught me.
I am every tear I wept and every smile I smiled,
I am every pain and every joy that touched me,
I am also every heart that was touched by my pain, touched by my laughter.

I am ageless.
I am every leaf I touched, every flower I smelled and every path I walked,
I am every dish I ate and every wine I drank.
I am all those moments I savoured and all I savoured with.
I am every song I sang and all the lyrics I heard,
I am in every tune and every tune is in me.

I am ageless.
I am more than the sum of all my parts.
Moving on, I do so on the wings of a prayer,
May life continue to soak me in its joy

Drop by Drop.

Acknowledgements

I am grateful to so many people who are part of my life and have contributed in one way or the other to who I am.

My deepest gratitude to my guru and exemplar, Pandit Rajmani Tigunait, who has taught me most by example. His life-affirming teachings, distilled wisdom and boundless joy have greatly influenced me. And I know that it is in his allowing that I stand before him and learn.

My gratitude to my teachers, Ishan Tigunait and Sue Knight, who gave me the skills to understand the language of the mind.

It has been my fortune to have my mother's voice guide me to always listen to my inner teacher. This is essentially the spirit the book carries.

My children's love and enthusiasm as I wrote the book will always warm my heart.

My gratitude to my editor, Ruchika Chanana, who placed her faith in my writing and gave me the confidence I needed to put my work out. And for carefully guarding my voice and letting it stay intact, while gently encouraging me to find my own refinements.

Acknowledgements

I will always remain thankful to some special people who took the time and interest to participate in this journey with me. Anupama Sawhney, Shibani Chopra, Sonya Sapru, Sonalee Kumar: your love and support will continue to breathe through the pages of this book. And to Radhika Kukreja, Rita Bakshi and my other dear friends and family who have been with me even in their silence.

And finally, my gratitude to the greatest protagonist of all: Life.

Bibliography

Solnit, Rebecca. *A Field Guide to Getting Lost*. New York: Viking, 2005.

Rilke, Rainer Maria, 1875-1926. *Letters to a Young Poet*. San Rafael, Calif. : New World Library, 1992.

Stryker, Rod. *The Four Desires*. London: Hay House, 2012.

Busch, Akiko. *How to Disappear*. USA: Penguin, 2020.

Audrey Hepburn. *Icon of Our Times*. Bath: International Book Marketing Bath, 2009.

Tigunait, Pandit Rajmani. *The Secret of the Yoga Sutra, Samadhi Pada*. Himalayan Institute Press, 2014.

Wilber, Ken. *No boundary: Eastern and Western approaches to personal growth*. Boulder, Colo: Shambhala, 1981.

Tigunait, Pandit Rajmani. *The Secret of the Yoga Sutra, Sadhana Pada*. Himalayan Institute Press, 2017.

Watts, Alan W. *The Wisdom of Insecurity*. New York: Vintage Books, 1951.

De Botton, Alain. *The Course of Love*. New York: Grove Press, 2015.

You Tube talks by Dan Gilbert and Alan W. Watts.

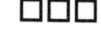

NOMITA KAPUR lives in New Delhi, India. Hers is a landscape grown rich by a deeper immersion in various facets of her universe. An alumnus of the Delhi School of Economics, she began her career in the corporate sector. Always interested in human behaviour, she soon forayed into being a corporate trainer and thereafter a professor of Organizational Behavior. Along with deepening her academic interests, she currently studies the scriptures of Indian philosophy under the guidance of her spiritual teacher.

Playing her various roles as a householder she has led a full life. An avid traveller, a drummer at heart with a keen interest in music, she is a citizen of our global world but remains deeply rooted the ethos of her own culture. This is her first work of writing, coming as a culmination of her own journey of self-inquiry. Nomita's endeavour is to access the eternal truths and attempt to bring them into contemporary life.

Having taught and trained individuals across age groups, she now shares her love for teaching through her writing and meditation coaching.

She can be reached at nomita@yagaliving.com